Organisations
and
Development

Organisations
and
Development

Strategies, Structures and Processes

REIDAR DALE

Sage Publications
New Delhi/Thousand Oaks/London

First published in 2000 by

Sage Publications India Pvt Ltd
M-32 Market, Greater Kailash, Part 1
New Delhi 110 048

Sage Publications Inc
2455 Teller Road
Thousand Oaks, California 91320

Sage Publications Ltd
6 Bonhill Street
London EC2A 4PU

Published by Tejeshwar Singh for Sage Publications India Pvt Ltd and printed at Chaman Enterprises, Delhi.

Library of Congress Cataloging-in-Publication Data

Dale, Reidar.
  Organisations and development: strategies, structures and processes/by Reidar Dale.
      p. cm.   (cl.)   (pbk.)
    Includes bibliographical references and index.
    1. Non-governmental organizations. 2. Economic development. 3. Rural development. I. Title.
    HD82.D295   338.9'0068—dc21   2000   00-033278

ISBN: 0–7619–9429–7 (US–HB)   81–7036–942–8 (India–HB)
          0–7619–9430–0 (US–PB)   81–7036–943–6 (India–PB)

Sage Production Team: Jaya Chowdhury, Mathew P.J. and Santosh Rawat

CONTENTS

LIST OF FIGURES, TABLES AND BOXES

FIGURES

TABLES

BOXES

FOREWORD

This is an important topical book – small but not lightweight, broad-based but not meandering, focused but not narrow. It is a deep well of innovative development thought, but not a bottomless pit. The book provides admirably easy access to a dauntingly difficult agenda – designed as a true guide and source book, rather than a simplifying 'how to' manual.

Reidar Dale writes from the vantage point of his dual career (which I believe to be the only sensible one for an academic in this field). After many years of practical experience as 'field worker', project manager and evaluator, he has built his academic reputation by helping the young professionals at the Asian Institute of Technology to find their way between theory and practice in a field which may well be described by the title of this book – Organisations and Development. It is the little 'and' in the title which is most significant, representing the critical linkage between development goals (above all, eradication of poverty and deprivation) and the organisational framework for doing development work. This particular angle makes this book such a valuable contribution, as not much has been written about that linkage, except perhaps for the growing literature on democratic decentralisation and governance.

John Friedmann's 'linkage between knowledge and action' together with his 'empowerment' have always been my favourite definition of how 'planning' should take place in the political arena – critical and informed participatory action, which remains focused on agreed objectives. Throughout its carefully balanced six chapters, this book provides a similarly structured linkage between means and ends of development, in the context of the broad organisational environment in which any objective-oriented action is supposed to happen.

Not long ago, feasibility studies and other development planning documents had a chapter added on at the end, with a title like 'institutional framework' or 'administrative setting'. Many times, otherwise technically sound project work, including heavy capital investment, failed miserably as the responsible agencies and any donors woke up to the sobering recognition that they had not paid enough attention to the sticky problem behind that last chapter. The afterthought to the project document should have been the centrepiece of the entire work. Any development action is doomed to fail unless the institutional environment is well understood.

'Organisation' is the author's short-hand for structures and processes of governance, comprising the state, the civil society and the market. He addresses development primarily in a rural setting, without narrowing the focus to the spatial framework of small communities and their economic microcosm. That would not reflect the reality of the so-called developing countries, where the rural sphere interlocks with an increasingly urban one, being also linked with the global market forces.

I have happily accepted the honour and pleasure of writing a foreword, because I share most of Reidar Dale's views and some of his experience. Having learned a great deal from my colleague's insight into links between means and ends and dimensions of organisation, I would wish the book the broadest possible readership among students, professionals and trainers, to support them in their efforts for competent development work through more thoroughly understood and better designed organisation.

Hans Detlef Kammeier

Professor of Urban and Regional Planning
Asian Institute of Technology

PREFACE

This book is about organised development work. After exploring the concept of development itself, I specify types of organisations in the development field and present views on their role and performance; discuss main concepts, dimensions and issues of development strategy and strategy formulation; address a range of organisational dimensions and issues; explore the concepts and dimensions of participation and capacity-building; and suggest frameworks and approaches for evaluating development organisations and their work.

The overall purpose of the book is to present and discuss a range of concepts, dimensions and issues of development strategy and organisation that I think all students and practitioners in the development field should be familiar with, be able to reflect conscientiously on, and be competent to apply or address constructively in their respective pursuits.

The issues of deprivation and development which are conceptualised in the first chapter and further reflected on subsequently are most typical of less developed societies. However, most topics addressed and perspectives applied are not restricted to any specific societal setting; the analysis should, thus, have broad relevance across societies.

The book covers a broad field and emphasises relations between dimensions of strategy and organisation rather than in-depth exploration of specific topics and issues. For further analysis of these, the reader is guided to more specialised literature.

The many inter-connections between categories and variables are highlighted by extensive cross-referencing, in the main text and in footnotes.

Within this broad framework, I provide innovative perspectives and interpretations on several more specific topics. Examples are: a typology of development organisations, perspectives on strategy formulation, a typology of organisational forms in the development field, co-ordination mechanisms relating to development work, and certain aspects of evaluation.

The broad scope may perhaps be difficult to relate to for some readers and may even irritate a few. There are long conceptual distances between, for instance, general notions of development, forms of development organisations, conceptions of empowerment, and dimensions of strategic planning. This breadth of topics and issues, at the expense of deep exploration of a narrower set of them, is considered to be justified on the following main grounds:

- it promotes recognition and understanding of numerous relations in development work that are commonly little regarded;
- it helps to make students of development aware of and sensitive to the scope of organisation-related topics and issues that development work involves.

On these grounds, the reader's acceptance is requested of the obvious fact that not every topic and issue explored may be shown to be directly linked with each and every other topic and issue that are addressed in the book.

Partly related, each chapter constitutes a fairly clearly bounded entity. This should in itself be a main advantage of the book, in that it enables the reader to study the chapters in any sequence, or even to concentrate on one chapter only, particularly when making use of the mentioned cross-references to connected topics and issues in other chapters.

Still, I recommend that persons who intend to read the whole book do so from beginning to end, in order to make the process smoother and facilitate the understanding of arguments.

The book has largely been developed from teaching material which I have worked out for university-level courses that I have taught in development analysis, planning and management. It is written primarily in response to a need I and my students have felt for a relatively basic and broad-focusing textbook on strategy analysis and organisation in the development field.

I would expect the book to serve this textbook purpose in the disciplines of development studies, planning and administration, as well as in development focused courses within more basic social sciences, such as sociology, political science and geography.

The book should also be useful for trainers and trainees of a range of short courses on development related topics, for professionals of development organisations, and for planners and managers of development programmes and projects.

In order to make the book suitable and attractive for such a broad and varied readership, I have avoided heavy academic language and have illuminated the presentation through numerous illustrations.

Chapter One

CONCEPTUALISING DEVELOPMENT

1. GROWTH AND DEVELOPMENT

Growth is used here in an economic sense, synonymously with 'economic growth'. It means, generally speaking, an increase in the amount of economic goods (commodities and services) that are produced in a society per individual or household of that society and a concomitant increase in the inhabitants' ability to acquire economic goods.

Development is a broader and more diverse concept, denoting improvements in the quality of life of people, extending much beyond direct gains from increased production of commodities and services.

The dominant view has been that economic growth in a society, if sustained over a sufficiently long period, would ensure gradual improvements in the quality of life of virtually all the people living in the society. This would occur through:

- transfer of growth from some core production units and economic sectors to other units and sectors;

- transformation of the economic surplus from increased production into increased income for the people who get incorporated into the growth process, starting with those who first exploit new production opportunities (the entrepreneurs) and spreading to other sections of the population;

- transformation of the increased income into broader economic and social welfare.

Some have thought that such changes would and should occur primarily through the workings of the market forces, others that they would need to be promoted through active support and regulation by the state, and yet others that they would have to be directly planned and implemented by agencies of the state.

Now, development analysts agree that there has been substantial economic growth in many countries without significant improvements in the quality of life of large numbers of people. Commonly, the majority of the population has continued to live under miserable economic and social conditions, and the living situation of many people has even worsened.

One has come to realise more than earlier that improvements in people's quality of life depend on many factors beyond economic growth in the society, of political, social, cultural and environmental nature.

It is now also widely recognised that growth, unless it is monitored and influenced by some institutions that are not driven by profit motives – in practice largely by state institutions – may lead to more unequal living conditions, nationally and internationally, and that it may have a range of adverse effects on the natural environment.

Simultaneously, economic growth may be necessary for development; i.e., augmentation of human welfare may require that the stock of economic goods (material and non-material) at the disposal of societies increases.

Different views on societal changes may be clarified more by juxtaposing basic *ideologies* of development. Based on factors which have commonly been perceived as essential for inducing changes, we may distinguish between three major ideologies, each of which encompasses numerous more specific ideologies and theories of growth and development. Briefly sketched, these main perspectives on development are:

Development as a spontaneous process

This may be termed the liberal ideology. Growth is here viewed as something natural, occurring through the workings of the *market forces*. It becomes a *self-inducing* process, because people, wanting improvements for themselves, respond to economic stimuli by producing and/or consuming more or by changing the composition of the commodities and services that are produced and consumed.

People's desire for commodities and services is expressed as *demand*. Producers will try to satisfy that demand, i.e., to *supply* what people want. As they do so, they may need production inputs from other enterprises and their own income will increase, leading to additional demand for various goods on their part. This triggers, in turn, increased supply from yet others, and so on.

The *price mechanism*, as operating in a relatively free market, is thought to regulate the allocation of resources optimally, balancing supply and demand at any time.

However, there are *hindrances* against growth of various sorts, such as physical, social and cultural barriers. Removing such hindrances should be a major role of the state in the development process.

Growth will not only trickle down to all sections of the population, but will also be converted into increased welfare for individuals, because people are considered to be able and free to make rational choices for improving their welfare and able to use increased resources effectively to that end. This ideology can therefore be perceived as a *harmony view* of development.

Moreover, all countries are expected to follow *the same general path* of growth and development.

Development as a state-planned process

An alternative view has been that growth and development must be *engineered* and *directed* through state planning.

This perspective has been most strongly manifested in *communist* societies. A core feature of the communist ideology is that the production technology and the relation between those involved in production are seen as determinants (the material basis) for societal institutions, social structures and people's welfare. A major conflict is seen as existing between, on the one hand, the owners of the means of production and some allies they may have and, on the other hand, the labourers – usually called the 'proletariat'.

State planning is linked to this notion of class conflict: growth and development can only encompass the masses and become sustained after a revolution which makes the state the representative of the proletariat and the steering agent of societal change. State planning may be highly centralised or more decentralised.

The recent collapse of the Soviet Union has widely discredited the highly centralised communist model, in particular.

Intermediate perspectives

Social-democratic theories advocate strong but more selective state intervention, in a setting of mainly private ownership of the means of production. The associated political ideology has, in somewhat varying forms, characterised West European countries for long and has exerted influence much more widely.

Social-democratic ideology emphasises the role of the state as a *facilitator* and *regulator* of change and a *re-distributor* of wealth, re-channelling money and other resources to social programmes, weak population groups, peripheral areas, etc. More lately, the state has also come to be seen as an *environment protector*, i.e., a guarantor against destruction of the natural environment through human activities, most of which are usually production-related.

Analysts have also emphasised the role of the state in promoting rapid growth in Japan and, subsequently, in other basically market orientated economies in East and Southeast Asia. Here, it has been particularly active in stimulating and regulating capital and commodity markets.[1]

---

[1]   Among the large number of writings on development theories, I propose Hunt (1989) for a good overview.

The role and workings of the state will be addressed more in Chapter Two.

2. CONVENTIONAL INDICATORS OF DEVELOPMENT

ECONOMIC DIMENSION

Gross National Product

National accounting has served to produce the predominant measure of a country's total production, namely the *Gross National Product (GNP)*. The GNP is normally calculated for a year and commonly divided by the number of persons in the country (GNP per capita). It integrates such disparate items as agriculture, manufacturing industries, private services (professional and personal), and state services. The value of the production equals the market prices of the commodities and services or – when no genuine market price exists, such as for many public services – the cost of producing them.[2]

Increase in the GNP per capita has been widely used as the primary measure not only of growth but of development as well.

However, while being a good measure of growth and an essential concept for economic planning, the GNP has *shortcomings as a development indicator.*

First, the market values (or inferred values of non-marketed goods) expressed by the GNP may not conform well with perceived developmental values. That is, there may be very different opinions about how much economic goods (commodities and services) are worth in terms of added well-being for people who access them, although their monetary value (their price) may be fixed.

For marketed goods, economic values are determined by the relation between supply and demand. A major problem in this regard is that supply and demand (and therewith sales and purchases) are strongly influenced by the income distribution in the society. For instance, in a country with serious poverty, a rich person's annual

---

[2] The Gross Domestic Product (GDP) is a frequently used alternative measure to the GNP. The difference between the two is small for most countries.

expenses on one costly item, such as fuel for his or her car, may be much higher valued than the total annual outlay of a poor household for food and other essential items. So, rich people's expenditure contributes much to the GNP (assuming that all or much of this expenditure accrues as income to people in the persons' home country), while poor people's expenditure on necessities contributes relatively little.

Second, the GNP is a little reliable measure of subsistence production and production of other goods which are not sold and bought. The most widespread activities of this nature are cultivation or gathering of food items, etc. for own consumption, construction and maintenance of assets (such as houses) by the owners or users themselves, and informal services for other people. It is extremely difficult to get reliable information about the amounts of such goods that are produced, and the practice of measurement varies greatly. Additionally, domestic work and community services of various kinds are not at all incorporated in the GNP.

Third, and closely related, the value of commodities and services that are produced in the informal economy (goods that are produced in unregistered economic enterprises) tends to be grossly underestimated in official statistics, particularly in developing countries, where informal production is usually widespread.[3]

Fourth, the GNP does not or not fully account for certain negative consequences for people of production of various kinds. For instance, it disregards negative environmental effects of polluting and otherwise disturbing production and it does not distinguish between industries which use renewable resources and industries which deplete resources forever, in spite of the fact that such effects and depleting practices may substantially influence the well-being of groups of people, presently or in the future.

---

[3]   The concept of 'informal economy' (and the alternative one of 'informal sector') tends to be used with somewhat different meanings or with different degrees of specificity. The meaning given to it here corresponds with that of most economists, while anthropologists and sociologists may define the term more broadly, encompassing activities such as voluntary community work and production of goods for barter (direct exchange).

In addition, and most fundamentally, the GNP excludes a range of other non-economic welfare aspects. I will soon expand the horizon of analysis, incorporating such other aspects.

Widening the Perspective within an Economic Frame

First, however, let us have a quick look at some additional economic measures of growth and development.

A common supplement to the GNP per capita is the *income distribution* among people. A simple measure of this is the proportions of the national income which accrue to sections of the population, defined by the level of income (for instance, the 25 per cent of the households with the lowest income, the next 25 per cent, and so on).

Employment is another common measure. Main indicators are the distribution of the labour force across economic sectors and the proportion of work-seeking persons who are not employed (the rate of unemployment).

In less developed countries, in particular, the reliability of data for income distribution and employment tends to be low, due to inadequate recording systems, low incentives for people to report unemployment, and much part-time work.

More specific economic variables are also used as supplementary indicators. Examples, among many more, are:

- *electricity consumption*
- *newspaper reading*
- *automobile ownership*

These variables are calculated as the amount or number per capita or per a stated number of inhabitants. They may diversify the picture of economic performance and facilitate comparison between countries.

Moreover, economic growth, constituting an important part of most notions of development, particularly in less developed countries, requires that resources are withheld from consumption and diverted into investment. Therefore, a country's *capital formation* is calculated and used as a macro-economic planning tool by national economic planning agencies.

SOCIAL DIMENSION

Common social indicators of development are:

- *average expected life length at birth (life expectancy)*
- *infant mortality rate*
- *calorie consumption per capita*
- *proportion of under-nourished children*
- *hospital beds, usually per 1000 inhabitants*
- *literacy rate*
- *rate of enrolment in primary schools*
- *proportion of houses with piped water (mainly in urban areas)*
- *average number of persons per room (usually in urban areas)*

Some of the mentioned indicators denote *ends* of development, i.e., quality of life directly (for instance, life expectancy), whereas others denote *means* for improving the quality of life (for instance, hospital beds).

Some variables express some *distribution* in the population (for instance, the percentage of literate persons, commonly by sex) whereas others do not contain any notion of distribution (for instance, the average number of persons per room).

Such social indicators are measures of very important features of people's lives. Moreover, data pertaining to them are usually more reliable than most of the data which are produced on income and employment. That is largely because most such social indicators are more specific and, therewith, less difficult to define and delimit. This makes it easier to quantify them as well. Another reason is that governments are usually more directly in charge of many social services – most notably health and education services – than of economic production. This makes it easier for state agencies to record the situation in these fields.

ECONOMIC AND SOCIAL DIMENSIONS COMBINED

Comparing Indicators

Efforts are often made to compare indicators and sometimes even to compute the correlation between them. Most frequently, the GNP per capita of different countries is compared with social indicators for the same countries, such as life expectancy, child mortality and literacy.

The main idea is usually to see to what extent differences in national income between countries correspond with differences on social indicators between them.[4] .

Composite Indexes of Development

Efforts have also been made to combine economic and social indicators, i.e., to join them into some composite index, primarily for comparing the level of development of countries.[5]

Such broad-based indexes can be illustrative as general summaries for countries, as they may be more meaningful indicators of the level of development than the GNP per capita or the latter alone. Beyond that, they are hardly of much use, because they hide differences which may be essential for describing, understanding and explaining poverty and mechanisms of development. Showing different indicators separately is usually more informative.

---

[4]   International statistics, as compiled by UN agencies and the World Bank, in particular, show that countries with fairly similar low incomes have widely different values on social indicators. That is, at low levels of national income, other factors seem to be much more important than the total production in influencing social welfare. At higher levels of income, however, we can discern an association between the GNP per capita and social welfare, as expressed by the above mentioned indicators; i.e., countries with high national income also tend to have high social welfare.

[5]   For a brief overview of such indexes, see Alexander (1993). These include the Human Development Index, which has become a widely accepted and used indicator, particularly for comparison between countries.

3. POVERTY AND DEPRIVATION

Improving the quality of life of people who live in miserable conditions is the primary justification for development. For connecting human misery with development, we must be able to trace and understand mechanisms of generating and maintaining misery, which I will in the following refer to as 'poverty' and 'deprivation'.

In studying poverty and deprivation, we may apply general frameworks of analysis of wide relevance and applicability, as there are several common factors which tend to produce certain predominant features over most of the world.

However, more specific manifestations of poverty and deprivation and their causes vary much, between and within countries. We should, therefore, as far as possible analyse them in their specific settings and preferably at the level of the local community, the household or the individual.

Simultaneously, official poverty data are rarely readily available for such small units; they are usually aggregated for bigger geographical entities, such as countries, in order to give a general picture of the poverty situation and to support macro-planning.

DEFINING POVERTY

The term 'poverty' may be used in a fairly specific and narrow sense or with wider connotations. In its narrow sense, it is usually taken to denote the basic material condition of households or, less commonly, individuals, in terms of:

- *few and simple assets (for production and consumption)*
- *low income (in cash or in kind)*
- *low consumption*

Households with these characteristics commonly have a problem with the regularity of supply of income and food as well. We may, therefore, also incorporate:

- *variable supply of cash and food.*

BOX 1.1

GLIMPSES OF THE REALITY OF HUMAN MISERY

"1.3 billion of the world's population live on less than 9 dollars a day ... . Some 800 million people do not receive adequate food and nearly 500 million suffer from chronic malnutrition; 17 million people die each year from curable parasitic infections and diseases such as diarrhoea, malaria and tuberculosis ... . [In less developed countries] the infant mortality rate for children under five is almost six times greater than the rate in developed countries.

There has been a marked increase in the number of poor people whose income has actually declined ... . Over the past 30 years the income of the poorest 20 per cent of the world's people declined from 2 per cent to 1.45 per cent of the global income.

... 30 per cent of the global labour force [is] unemployed or underemployed. Prolonged unemployment leads to ... increased apathy, a serious loss of interest in socialising and a gradual withdrawal from the labour force. Loss of self-esteem is a defining element.

Global poverty continues to affect women and children especially. Forced by circumstances, children account for a growing proportion of the labour force ... and work under deplorable conditions of exploitation. The problem of street children has become more widespread ... and poor children have become a target of choice for drug traffickers.

The severe social tensions that have been building up provide a fertile breeding ground for processes that weaken the social fabric. These include the breakdown of the family and rising criminality.

Together, these deficiencies are creating vicious circles ... Nutritional deficiencies in early childhood, the absence of a stable family setting, limitations on attending and remaining in school, and marginalisation from the labour market give rise to a situation of social exclusion which is self-perpetuating."

Source: Kliksberg (1997)

In national and international statistics on poverty, the emphasis is usually on income and consumption.

Wider definitions of 'poverty' may encompass some or all of the categories that will be addressed in the following few pages. I will, however, along with Robert Chambers (1983; 1995), refer to such wider conceptions of human misery and disadvantages as 'deprivation' rather than 'poverty'.

ABSOLUTE AND RELATIVE POVERTY

Before examining such additional features, we should clarify the concepts of 'absolute poverty' and 'relative poverty', commonly used in literature.

Absolute poverty means that the minimum material requirements for sustaining a decent life are not fulfilled; in other words, *basic material needs* are not met. The usual question posed is whether a household has sufficient income to purchase a 'basket' of basic commodities for consumption or, alternatively, produces these commodities itself.

The level at which basic material needs are considered to be just met is commonly referred to as the *poverty line*. In this perspective, then, the poor people are those who fall below that line.

The proportion of the households of a country or region which falls below the poverty line is a common measure of the degree of poverty in the population of that country or region.

The basket of commodities that may be considered as necessities varies between societies. This makes comparisons less accurate.

In developing countries, it is usually also difficult to get reliable information about household income and consumption, unless it is acquired through detailed surveys. Since such surveys may be undertaken for relatively small groups of people only, the inaccuracies may be great for larger populations (such as the entire population of a country).

Relative poverty denotes the material living condition of individuals or households in a society *compared* with the condition of other individuals or households in that society or compared with some subjective judgement of what is 'adequate'.

For example, a relative *poverty line* for households in a country may be set at one half of the average income of households in the country. Or, it may be based on some poll, where people are asked to tell what they think is a minimum income for leading a decent life. The degree of relative poverty of that country would then be the proportion of the population which falls below such a line.

One can not, of course, make direct comparison of relative poverty between societies.

Besides distinguishing between people below and above a poverty line, we may talk of *degrees of poverty* of those living below the line. One common measure is the 'poverty gap', denoting how far below the line the average income of the poor households is. In statistical documents, the gap is computed according to some formula, using available income data. With Chambers (1983), we can give more human content to this concept by distinguishing between:

- *the desperate*: people struggling with day-to-day survival;
- *the vulnerable*: people struggling to meet any extraordinary or unexpected (contingent) needs in whatever way;
- *the dependent*: people struggling to meet daily and contingent needs without humiliation.

ROBERT CHAMBERS' DEPRIVATION TRAP

According to Chambers (1983), *deprived households* usually have similar basic characteristics. Such households tend to be:

- *poor:*
  having few and simple assets; having inadequate and unreliable supplies of cash and food; and being continually indebted;
- *physically weak:*
  with members having poor health; with frequent births and deaths; with a high ratio of dependants to able-bodied adults; and with its members continually pressed for time and energy;

- *isolated:*

  living far away from centres of communication and information; participating little in public meetings; being little informed about events beyond their neighbourhood; and receiving no or few visits by extension workers etc.;

- *vulnerable:*

  having little resistance against unexpected or occasionally occurring unfavourable events, which often forces them to incur more debt or to sell or mortgage assets;

- *powerless:*

  being ignorant of the law; getting little advise; competing for employment or services with others in the same situation; having little power to negotiate the terms for its labour or the price for its products; avoiding political activity which might endanger future employment or protection; and being easily exploited by moneylenders, merchants, landlords, officials and the police.

These features of deprivation tend to be *interrelated*. That is, they interact and re-enforce each other in producing and maintaining deprivation. Chambers refers to this situation as a *deprivation trap*.

A FURTHER ELABORATION OF 'DEPRIVATION'

Below, I elaborate common features of deprivation somewhat further. Most of the categories correspond quite well with those of Chambers, but they are structured slightly differently. I have, in addition, incorporated more explicitly basic mind-related features, and I express more directly poor health and illiteracy as aspects of deprivation.

Some of these features (for instance, illiteracy and indebtedness) may be identified and specified fairly easily. Others are less directly observable and often tend to be overlooked. However, they may be crucial aspects of a person's or a household's well-being.

The categories incorporated here are additional to the poverty categories presented a couple of pages back.

- *poor health*,
  reducing directly people's quality of life and limiting initiative
  and the ability to work;
- *lack of formal education and illiteracy*,
  limiting people's access to information and ideas;
- *little communication with important persons or organisations*,
  reducing people's access to information, various kinds of services, and benefits of government programmes;
- *little participation in decision-making about societal affairs*,
  limiting the ability of poor people to influence directions of development, including factors that may affect them directly;
- *low receptiveness to mental stimuli*,
  being common for people whose main concern is their struggle
  for day-to-day living in a material sense, influencing negatively
  their attention to new ideas and the ability to make changes in
  their life;
- *structural weakness of household*,
  main manifestations of which may be a high ratio of dependants to people who earn, frequent births and deaths, and members not being able to organise well the use of their time and resources – all having negative consequences for the household's
  ability to cope with challenges that it faces;
- *competition among the poor for scarce resources*,
  reducing the bargaining power of the poor and their access to
  basic means of livelihood;
- *indebtedness*
  of an exploitative nature, which may tie up the use of a person's
  or household's material resources;
- *subordination*,
  aspects of which may be dependency on others on unfavourable
  terms for food or money, cultural subordination, and gender

subordination – being direct expressions of suffering as well as debilitating factors in many respects;

- *vulnerability,*

  meaning that persons or households have low resistance against unexpected or occasional unfavourable events, because they lack reserves – which may be of material or non-material nature – for tackling them;

- *enduring mental or physical violence,*

  from individuals (such as husbands) and organised units (such as sections of the state), being a deprivation of potentially very severe nature;

- *mental distress*

  caused by repressive actions or difficulties in one's environment, being a directly felt deprivation which may override virtually any other, if strong enough;

- *low self-esteem,*

  being a frequent human reaction to the mentioned factors, commonly coupled with a state of apathy regarding one's situation.

The above express, of course, *general tendencies* for disadvantaged individuals and households. In real situations, different characteristics are manifested to various degrees in different combinations, while some may be absent altogether.

The mentioned categories may be *interrelated* in various ways and to different extents. There is also an amount of overlap between some of them. Features of deprivation are rarely individual problems and can seldom be solved in isolation.

These features are inter-woven with various aspects of *social differentiation,* such as inequality by class, caste, education and gender. Some of these may be directly expressed by our concept of subordination, others less directly so.

The political, legal, administrative, economic and social arrangements of societies tend to be weighted against deprived people. That is, such people tend to live and work within systems which have been created by influential people, and which often primarily serve their own interests.

Persons and households who have lived in deprivation for many years or generations, tend not to seriously question their situation, but to accept it as something inescapable. They have, then, adapted to a *survival strategy* and may have no aim in their life which may be called a development objective.

4. A FURTHER ELABORATION OF 'DEVELOPMENT'

'Development' was in the beginning of the chapter loosely defined as 'improvements in the quality of life of people'.

As substantiated above, quality of life involves much more than what may be quantified by the earlier mentioned economic and social indicators of development. We need to deepen our perception of 'development' beyond these overt economic and social features, to include less visible and more complex features and relations. These may be direct expressions of characteristics of individuals and households or they may be features of the wider society.

DIRECTLY PEOPLE-RELATED DIMENSIONS

Reflecting the features of deprivation which have been mentioned in previous pages, I will categorise such additional aspects of development as:

- *orientation of the mind:*
  perception of one's own position and opportunities in the society, being closely related to whether or to what extent one has a development strategy (as opposed to a survival strategy) for oneself and one's dependants;

- *dependent versus independent position:*
  degree and terms of indebtedness, degree of competition for scarce resources, degree of inequality in gender relations, etc. –

influencing the degree of freedom in making choices about aspects of one's life;

- *marginalised versus integrated position:*
  degree and terms of participation in markets, degree and terms of participation in political and social life, type and strength of economic and social security networks;

- *degree of freedom from physical and mental violence:*
  the extent to which one may lead one's life without deliberate maltreatment or fear of such maltreatment, within one's family and in the wider society;

- *degree of mental satisfaction:*
  the degree of mental peace and the ability to enrich one's life through non-material stimuli.

'Orientation of the mind' is sometimes referred to as the *perceptional* dimension of development.

Major features of the dimensions of 'dependent–independent' and 'marginalised–integrated' are sometimes referred to as the *political* dimension. Embedded in this concept is, normally, democratisation, in a wide sense. However, as the word 'political' is ambiguous and often used in a more narrow sense, I prefer to refer to these dimensions along with the degree of freedom from violence as *structural* or *relational*.

Relations of dependency may be exploitative, welfare promoting, or more neutral in this respect. Highly industrialised societies are characterised by strong dependencies and interdependencies of various kinds, both economic and social, which need not be exploitative. But numerous dependency relations may be of highly exploitative nature, commonly more so in less developed societies than in so-called welfare societies.

The category of 'marginalised–integrated' embeds essential elements of society-connected welfare (as reflected in the term 'welfare societies'), i.e., the extent to which people can rely on help from societal institutions in situations of distress.

ADDITIONAL SOCIETAL DIMENSIONS

The above mentioned features relating to individuals and/or house-holds can be added up and translated into categories pertaining to whole societies, meaning how typical, frequent or strong the various features are in a society.

Moreover, at any level in any society, the mentioned categories are intertwined with:

- *institutional features of societies:*
  laws and other legal institutions; organisation of political life; scope, range and importance of public and private development organisations; orientation, effectiveness and efficiency of public administration; institutional mechanisms for sustainable use of natural resources; etc.

We need to always be conscious that issues of development are normative; that is, they are reflections of personal and societal values. Consequently, different people may attach different importance to different aspects, and the prioritisation may be influenced by political system, religion and cultural tradition.

To all the above mentioned dimensions come additional changes in the society, during a process of growth and development, which may be considered as less normative or non-normative (i.e., changes which in themselves are not desirable or not obviously so). We may, therefore, refer to them as *other societal changes* rather than additional dimensions of development. Main such changes, having been closely related to economic growth and development everywhere, are:

- *economic differentiation* (increased specialisation of production and a closely related expansion of trade between production units);
- *urbanisation* (an increase in the proportion of the population living in urban areas);
- *reduced fertility* (fewer children per woman of child-bearing age).

TABLE 1.1

CHARACTERISTICS OF HIGHLY DEVELOPED SOCIETIES
A Broad Interpretation

<u>Economic</u>

High income per capita
High income equality
Little unemployment
High savings ratio

Directly welfare-
expressing

More indirectly
connected to
welfare

<u>Social</u>

Low child mortality
High average life length
Little malnourishment
High literacy rate
High rate of school enrolment
Widespread access to basic housing and sanitary amenities

<u>Perceptional</u>

Development attitudes predominant

<u>Mental welfare</u>

Little mental distress
Wide opportunities for mental and intellectual enrichment

<u>Relational</u>

Freedom from mental and physical violence
Freedom from exploitative dependency relations
High social security
High rate of participation in societal affairs

<u>Institutional</u>

Human rights-promoting laws and rules
Participation-promoting political system
Freedom to organise to promote one's own and others' welfare
Effective and efficient public administration
Good health services for all
Basic education services for all
Wide opportunities for advanced education

A SUMMARY

Based on the presentation above I have, in Table 1.1, endeavoured to summarise main characteristics of societies that we may consider as relatively highly developed. The last-mentioned, non-normative aspects are not included in the table.

A distinction is made between features that express welfare directly and features that are more appropriately considered as means in development. The former are italicised in the table.

Development being a highly normative concept, the set of categories incorporated is, of course, subjective. Moreover, the importance attached to each of the categories appearing in the table may differ substantially, between societies and between individuals in the same society. There may, for example, be differences between the genders in the rating of features of importance, in some societies more than in others, and well-informed persons may have a broader perspective on dimensions and alternatives than those who are less well informed.

Equality and democracy in broad senses are basic values on which much of the typology is based.

5. MODES OF ANALYSIS

By the scope of investigation, we may, with reference to our framework, distinguish between two main types of analysis of poverty, deprivation and development: 'intra-category' and 'relational'.

With *intra-category analysis* I mean limiting the study to one of the poverty, deprivation or development components that have been presented (or similar components). Examples may be consumption, indebtedness, mental distress, literacy rate, education services and health services.

A predominant feature of intra-category analysis is that it tends to be descriptive only or primarily so, because one usually needs to look beyond the category itself to find explanatory factors for observations. If our analytical categories are broad enough, certain aspects may be explained by internal relations, for instance, deficiencies in one part of a health provision system by deficiencies in other parts of that system. Simultaneously, all the deficiencies may be more fundamentally linked to category-external factors.

By *relational analysis* I mean

(a) study of person–person and person–institution connections, referred to as the 'relational' category in our deprivation and development framework (see, for instance, the table);

(b) analysis of links between categories of this framework, between parts of different categories, and between such categories or sub-categories and any other societal feature.

Due to the high complexity that usually characterises societal phenomena, relational analysis is usually needed to provide good understanding of an issue that is studied.

These two types (intra-category and relational) are partly connected to the methods of analysis. At the most general level, a basic distinction is often made between 'quantitative' and 'qualitative'. This distinction relates to both collection, processing, documentation and any other form of presentation of data and information.[6]

Here, I will not delve into questions of data and information collection, but briefly address main means of *processing* what has been collected and the corresponding *presentation* of information.[7] In this perspective, we may broadly distinguish between four kinds of analysis, with different strengths and weaknesses, being described and discussed over the next few pages.

---

[6]   For a more detailed but still compact presentation and examination of quantitative and qualitative approaches than is given here, see Dale (1998). That book also contains references to other literature that examines the topic in greater depth.

[7]   A brief overview of methods of generating data and information for the purpose of evaluation is given at the end of Chapter Six. Dale (1998) elaborates the topic somewhat further and makes references to more specialised literature.

Direct numerical measurement is normally the most specific form of analysis. Collected data are processed quantitatively and the resulting information is expressed by numbers. It corresponds to what is commonly referred to as measurement on ratio and interval scales, in both discrete and continuous form.[8]

Because numerical data are specific and usually readily understood, and due to their ability to express comparison in unambiguous and summary terms, most of us have an inclination to present messages in numerical form whenever possible.

The major problem with this is that only some overt features of human deprivation and development may be expressed in such form. They are, generally, those that are found in statistical documents, such as income, calorie intake and literacy rate. Less readily discernible or definable features of deprivation and numerous dimensions of development can not be given numerical expression.

Closely linked, if we limit our analysis of poverty, deprivation and development to what may be quantified, we are often not able to explain much. Explanations of these phenomena are normally complex, while a quantitative design places strong restrictions on what may be explored and how one may do it. Consequently, in quantitative analysis, relations between variables tend to be grossly simplified. Often, they are expressed by a single number only, such as the correlation coefficient, or by an either–or statement, for instance, whether or not a detected association between two variables is statistically significant.[9]

---

[8]   The ratio scale has an absolute (non-arbitrary) zero, while the interval scale does not have it. A discrete variable has clearly separated values appearing in 'steps' (such as 1, 2, 3), while the values on continuous variables may in principle be endlessly subdivided (for instance, by decimal numbers).

[9]   For a more elaborate and intriguing argument, see Chambers (1993).

Of course, we must distinguish between, on the one hand, the simplicity that tends to characterise the outcome of quantitative analyses relating to development, such as associations and cause-effect relations, and, on the other hand, the high level of sophistication and the complexity of many statistical methods which are applied to produce that outcome.

Category-level measurement corresponds to what is commonly referred to as measurement at the ordinal and nominal levels (on ordinal and nominal scales). At the nominal level, observations are grouped into named categories. In ordinal-level measurement, one ranks the observations by some specified criterion (such as magnitude or importance).

An example, in our sphere, of nominal-level measurement may be the placing of households below or above a poverty line (as defined earlier). An example of ordinal-level measurement may be the ranking of households by their degree of poverty or deprivation, usually by grouping them into a set of pre-specified categories. Our categorisation, a few pages back, of people by their level of deprivation, as the 'desperate', the 'vulnerable' and the 'dependant', is a measure of poverty at the ordinal level.

This is basically a weaker form of measurement than numerical measurement, and it may enable equally little or even less explanation.

However, category-level measurement may be useful in that it may enable systematic summary of certain kinds of qualitative information, otherwise basically and more comprehensively analysed in the verbal mode (see immediately below). Commonly, therefore, it may be seen primarily as a helping tool in basically qualitative pieces of analysis rather than an analytical method of much merit in its own right.

Verbal statements have the opposite strengths and weaknesses to those of measurements. Such statements are, usually, less specific expressions, while they carry, potentially, a virtually endless ability to link and explain. However, the extent to which verbal statements differ from numerical ones varies hugely, demonstrating the enormous flexibility of written words and sentences as an analytical tool.

For producing information about poverty, deprivation and development that goes beyond plain descriptive or explanatory expressions in summary form, verbal statements are normally needed.

BOX 1.2

EMPOWERMENT THROUGH ORGANISATION

"In an analysis of features and impacts of such a programme one needs to consider aspects of the structure of power, the distribution of resources, and the decision-making processes which influence the control of and access to resources by the rural population. In the present context, as typically in rural societies in poor countries, access to land and related resources and the terms and conditions of such access are crucial. These factors constitute much of the basis for the social structure and are commonly the primary source of power for the rural elite. This land based elite determines terms of relations between people which are crucial to the persistence of poverty. Another feature is the structure of the markets ... . The intermediaries who largely control [the markets] ... [gain] substantial power ... over resources and their distribution. The merchants, money lenders, and village traders are the main intermediaries. Commonly, one person performs more than one of these roles."

"... [We have substantiated that] Group and Society members were able to elaborate on numerous causes of their poverty, emphasizing [a range of] factors ... . Exploitation of the poor in this context takes many forms. Crucial is dependence on financial capital on terms which the poor can not manage. Unable either to accumulate their own savings or obtain loans from established credit institutions, they must borrow from money lenders and merchants at very high interest rates. In order to secure such loans many have to mortgage their land and all too often lose it. They become sharecroppers, landless labourers, and even enter into labour relations which have features of bondage."

"... The study has documented impressive improvements in various aspects of the lives of the intended beneficiaries of the programme, and has corroborated that these changes have to an overwhelming extent been induced by the programme.

Major directly observable effects of the process of change have been: release from indebtedness; improved housing, water supply and latrines; more household assets; and new production assets.

It is further evident that increased income and savings have been the most crucial direct factors behind the changes in the mentioned fields.

However, underlying and interwoven with these measurable changes have been continuous processes of mobilization, conscientization, and increasing organizational ability, by a combination of training and learning from own experience. Through these processes substantial changes have occurred in other intangible spheres as well: people's value systems have changed, their self-esteem has increased, and they have got an amount of bargaining power that they have hardly ever imagined could be possible. These factors, in turn, have triggered further material benefits."

Source: Iddagoda and Dale (1997)

Such statements are, therefore, by far the most used tool for analysing such societal phenomena (and most others).

Box 1.2 contains excerpts from a study by Iddagoda and Dale (1997) on a community organisation cum micro-finance programme. The case should illustrate well the widespread need for verbal analysis of issues of deprivation and development. No alternatives exist for describing and explaining societal structures and processes of such complex nature. The excerpts presented here are summary statements only; details of the analysis would further demonstrate the uniqueness of words and sentences for both description and explanation.

Still, in spite of the comprehensive need for it and its very widespread usage, and in spite of the intellectual challenge of good qualitative analysis, the verbal mode has been widely considered as inferior among scientists, including many scholars of many social sciences.

Words and sentences have, by these scientists, often been seen primarily as a supplement to the quantitative mode, mainly in terms of guiding the reader from one step of quantification to the next or as an alternative form of expressing or summarising a finding, rather than a means of analysis in its own right.

The tendency towards quantification in the social sciences has been closely linked to the scientific heritage of the natural sciences, connected to industrialisation and the associated technological development. A fear of social sciences being considered inferior to the natural sciences has also contributed.

However, the attitude to qualitative analysis is now becoming more positive in most social sciences.

It should also be emphasised that qualitative analysis has been the dominant or even the only form of analysis in parts of the development sciences, ever since these came to be recognised as a distinguishable discipline.

Graphical linking is another, much more specific, means of analysing poverty, deprivation and development. Basically, it is a tool for structuring certain qualitative information in a more concise and readily comprehensible form than may be done through verbal statements.

Thus, graphical linking has great limitations compared to verbal statements and is no substitute for them, but is a potentially useful supplement to some such statements.[10]

Graphical linking is exemplified by the flowchart in Figure 1.1.

The chart is influenced by a written story by Hartmann and Boyce, reproduced in Bernstein (1992).[11] With very few words, it illustrates how a household enters into deficiency of resources by

---

[10]   There are, of course, numerous other types of graphical presentations. Some, such as visual presentations of quantitative data, may be of even more supplementary nature. Others, such as mapping using geographical data, may be more substantial means of analysis.

[11]   Hartmann, B. and Boyce, J.K. (1983): *A Quiet Violence: view from a Bangladesh village*; Zed Books.

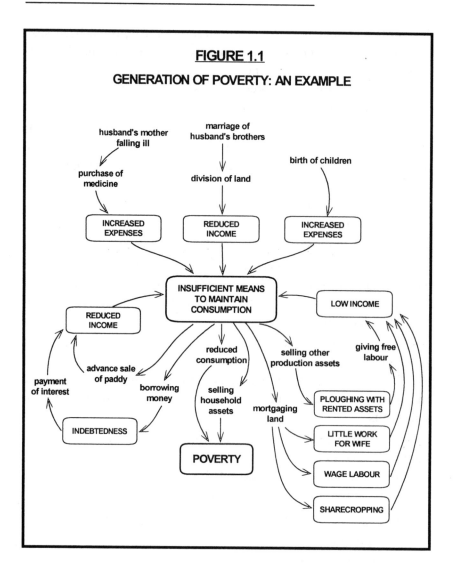

FIGURE 1.1

GENERATION OF POVERTY: AN EXAMPLE

three inducing factors: frequent purchase of medicine for a chroni-
cally ill household member, division of family land among the husband's brothers (at the time of their marriage), and the birth of many
children. It then shows how this resource deficiency leads the
household to adopt strategies for survival which keep it in a poverty
trap. The loops in the figure show what are commonly referred to as

'vicious circles of poverty' (see, for instance, Chambers [1983] and Burkey [1993]).

The chart is confined to variables of relatively overt nature, basically variables of poverty (as defined earlier in the present chapter) and factors directly connected to these poverty variables. It would be possible to conceptualise additional aspects of deprivation and to connect these to the present figure. Such additional factors might be linked to either the whole figure (which might then be considered as a poverty 'sub-system') or they might be linked to individual variables of the figure.

For instance, we might connect 'gender subordination' and 'mental distress' to certain variables or sets of variables (for which the story provides ample justification). We might also well consider each of the two loops that maintain poverty as constituting structures of 'subordination'.

Such visual presentations of links between variables that produce poverty and deprivation may help focus attention to key relations that may need to be broken for positive changes to occur in people's living situation. That is, negative relations and processes such as those shown in the figure may be juxtaposed to corresponding measures for promoting development.

In this case, measures to enhance income would be crucial, aiming at halting capital eroding practices, such as borrowing money (at high interest rates), selling paddy on root in advance (at only a fraction of the price for ripe harvested paddy), and selling and mortgaging assets. For breaking such vicious circles, some kind of inducement from outside may be needed, in direct or less direct form. Inducements may also come from planned changes in other but related spheres. In this and similar cases, examples of inducements may be: providing access to a new source of income, assistance for adopting new cultivation practices (to increase the productivity of land which may still remain at the poor households' disposal), and promoting loans on more favourable terms than poor people may obtain on the local capital market. Direct material assistance may also be coupled with non-material measures of less direct nature, such as an awareness-promoting campaign or the building of local organisations of deprived people.[12]

Similar relation charts (whether named flowcharts, relationship maps, cause-effect diagrams, or something else)[13] may be used to illustrate virtually any kinds of links between any kinds of variables that generate or maintain poverty, deprivation and development. However, there are strict limits to how complex and detailed one may make such diagrams before they become more heavy to read than a corresponding text.

> **Having, in this chapter, conceptualised 'development', connected this concept to the human problems that constitute its rationale (poverty and deprivation), and briefly reflected on how we may express these phenomena and related ideas, we are now ready to explore questions of how development may be promoted. The following chapters of the book will address this broad issue, in the perspective of strategies and numerous dimensions of organisation. First, in Chapter Two, we will focus attention on main types of organisations active in the development field and discuss their respective strengths and weaknesses.**

---

[12]   An example of a similar poverty situation and related measures is presented in Section 7 of Chapter Five.

[13]   For a simple overview of different types of charts, see Damelio (1996).

Chapter Two

ORGANISATIONS IN DEVELOPMENT

1. A TYPOLOGY OF DEVELOPMENT ORGANISATIONS

In contemporary societies, it is common to distinguish between three main institutional spheres: the *state*, the *civil society* and the *market*.

In all these spheres, organisations are formed and operate, although in some countries civil society organisations and private market organisations have been tightly circumscribed.

Most organisations of the state and the civil society are, by a frequently used term, non-profit bodies,[1] whereas organisations in the market sphere are business enterprises, aiming at generating profit for some individual person, group or institution (in some instances, the state).

Organisations within all these spheres contribute to development, in some sense, more or less directly. Here, however, we are concerned with development-focusing organisations within the spheres of the state and the civil society. The simple but fundamental reason for this delimitation is that these are organisations with a direct development mission, i.e., for which development constitutes the very purpose of existence.

---

[1] The concepts of 'non-profit' and 'non-profit organisation' are better defined and further elaborated in Section 5 of the present chapter.

I will, thus, define a <u>development organisation</u> as any *organised entity of society that contributes to development, as this was conceptualised in Chapter One, without aiming at generating profit for owners of the organisation from the work that it does.* [2]

Simultaneously, we must keep firmly in mind that it is business enterprises, of any size from the small farm to the multinational company, which generate the economic surplus on which much development depends, directly and more indirectly.

Organised units of the <u>state</u> may be broadly referred to as *political* and *administrative*. The former claim to represent the people within their geographical area of jurisdiction and should, consequently, be directly accountable to those people. The latter perform tasks that are specified, to larger or lesser extents, by policies, guidelines and regulations, the most general and important of which are supposed to be decided on by political bodies. Sometimes, however, the distinction between political and administrative roles may be blurred.

Moreover, an important distinction exists between the *central government* and *local governments*. The latter may be constituted at the local community or some intermediate level. Many bodies at intermediate levels are most appropriately referred to as 'regional' or 'provincial' governments. However, I will, for simplicity's sake, refer to all governmental bodies at sub-national levels with a substantial amount of autonomy (see Section 4) as local governments. Note, though, that in countries with a federal system, these are units below the 'state' level only.

---

[2]   Certain organisations that we may want to incorporate, aim at augmenting the members' income. See the next page for a further clarification of this.

More specific definitions may have to delimit development related activities and, therewith ,'development organisation' by many additional criteria. Main such criteria may be: the types of services offered, the kinds of technology promoted, and whether or the extent to which the organisation undertakes relief work. Such efforts at specification may easily become academic exercises with little practical applicability. The question will not be pursued further here.

The national government as a whole, bigger hierarchical entities within the central government (ministries), local governments and, possibly, some other state bodies consist of both politicians and administrators and perform roles that are defined for both the political and the administrative spheres.

In any local government area, there will normally be a combination of a) political and administrative units of the local government and b) administrative units of the central government, i.e., units at lower levels of hierarchically built government departments or other state agencies.

In an organisational perspective, the <u>civil society</u> is the sphere in which various kinds of voluntary movements emerge or get initiated and become structured.

The major common feature of most *civil organisations* is, as already stated, that they are non-profit entities.

An exception to this are many co-operative bodies which promote production and income of their members (being also their owners), but which are simultaneously based on a broader institutional ideology, including equality and member participation. For such entities to be referred to as civil society organisations, a delimiting criterion may be that the organisations themselves should not undertake production directly, at least as their main activity. If they do so, they should be considered as business enterprises, belonging to the market sphere.

Examples of income promoting organisations which may be considered to belong to the civil sphere are many savings and credit organisations, farmers' co-operatives and associations of industrialists.

Beyond this, civil organisations are hugely diverse, by overall purpose, interests, constituency, activities, etc. This diversity makes it very difficult to formulate any exhaustive organisational typology. Still, for various purposes, it is important to distinguish between organisations in the broad development sphere by some major characteristics. The following is an effort at some clarification.

A basic distinction is warranted between a) organisations made up of people who consider themselves to be the organisations' members, in a deep sense of 'membership', and which usually also render services to the members, and b) organisations without such a membership base, serving people outside themselves. The former may be referred to as *member organisations*, the latter as *service organisations*.

Uphoff (1986; 1996) emphasises the distinction between these two categories by referring to the arena of member organisations as the *voluntary sector* and that of service organisations as the *private sector*. The latter sector also encompasses private business organisations, as a separate sub-category.

The reason given by Uphoff for locating service organisations in the private rather than the voluntary sphere is that they serve external people, reminiscent of how business enterprises serve customers. The beneficiaries tend to be in a 'take it or leave it' relationship with the organisations that serve them and cannot hold them accountable for what they do in the same direct manner that members can of their own organisations (Uphoff [1996]: 25).

'Mutual benefit organisation' and 'public benefit organisation' are additional terms found in literature on civil organisations (see, for instance, Thomas [1992]). These terms are largely identical with 'member organisation' and 'service organisation' respectively. However, there are a few member organisations which wholly or primarily serve outsiders (an example of this at the international level being Amnesty International); these should, consequently, be referred to as public benefit organisations.

The above categorisation is presented in more compressed form in Table 2.1.

For a fuller perspective of the private sector, I have included private business enterprises in the table, although these are not considered as development organisations. Such enterprises may be owned by individuals or groups through a variety of arrangements, including some co-operative structure.

TABLE 2.1

ORGANISATIONS BY SOCIETAL SPHERE AND SECTOR

STATE	CIVIL SOCIETY		MARKET
Government Sector	**Voluntary Sector**		**Private Sector**
Central government Local government	Production related co-operatives	Non-profit organisations	Business enter-prises
Service organisations	Member organisations	Service organisations	
Public benefit organisations	Mutual benefit organisations	Public benefit organisations	

For an even fuller picture of organisations, governmental and semi-governmental business enterprises might have been included as well. In some countries state agencies are, at least formally, in charge of most production (although this has changed dramatically with the decline of orthodox communism); in other countries the government is in charge of key industries and/or regulates core production sectors or enterprises; and in yet other countries the role of the state in production is very limited.

'*People's organisation*' is a frequently applied term for member organisations. It may be used broadly, as encompassing all such organisations. Usually, however, it carries the notion of membership of and control by 'common' people, i.e., by non-professionals, in a conventional academic or technical sense. Member organisations of professionals within specific fields are also common, and are frequently referred to as *professional associations* or *unions*.

Most people's organisations with substantial direct influence by their members are of local nature. They are commonly referred to as *community-based organisations*. Such organisations vary with respect to relations with other organised units: they may be confined to one local community or a few adjoining communities, having no structured relations with any other bodies; they may be similar local organisations that may co-operate with each other, usually informally and commonly for specific purposes; or they may be bodies that are formally connected, by some kind of representation, to some higher-level body or bodies (tiers), being intended to serve the members' interests at the higher levels. In the latter case, one may refer to both the individual local bodies and the full set of tiered units as 'organisation', depending on the context and focus.

If such hierarchy-building becomes comprehensive, the influence of individual members may become highly indirect and sometimes negligible. An example is some co-operatives, which, from being locally based entities directly controlled by community inhabitants, have developed into highly bureaucratic bodies.

Other bodies that go by the name of co-operatives have not been initiated or even substantially influenced by their members, but are creations of governments. They are, then, statal rather than civil organisations.

A few community-based organisations may not be member-focused, but may instead work for the benefit of other people in their community. By our terminology, they are, then, service organisations.

However, the large majority of *service organisations* are bodies which work over larger areas than single local communities. On the basis of their geographical sphere of operation, they may be broadly referred to as regional, national and international organisations respectively.

Most service organisations of the civil society with a development orientation are usually called *non-governmental organisations (NGOs)* or *non-governmental development organisations (NGDOs)*. As commonly conceptualised and defined, they tend to have a well-specified mission,[3] they usually provide services that are considered as professional (requiring people with some specialised skills for rendering them), they have a clearly identifiable formal structure, they normally work with at least some salaried staff, and they often render support to other organisations (mostly community-based organisations, but also others, even governmental agencies).

NGDOs are of highly varying size, from small entities with a local focus, via units of different size with regional or national coverage, to big and complex international organisations. They may specialise in a narrowly defined field or cover a broader set of activities. Their work may be standardised or more varied and changeable, largely depending on their degree of flexibility in responding to specific problems, interests and development ideas in different localities and situations.[4]

It must also be mentioned that 'non-governmental organisation' is sometimes used with a broader meaning, even occasionally as encompassing all kinds of voluntary and private non-profit organisations. One also sees the term used without apparently any clear idea on the part of the writer or speaker of what it covers. Such broad or indiscriminate usage may create confusion and may constrains constructive analysis.[5]

---

[3] Definitions of 'mission' and other terms relating to the pursuits of organisations are given shortly, in Section 2.

[4] These and other dimensions of organisational strategy are analysed in Chapter Three.

[5] Many other efforts have been made to typify development organisations, although more selectively and in less specific terms than has been done here. Besides Uphoff (1986), referred to above, see, for instance, Eade (1997), Edwards and Hulme (eds.) (1996) and Thomas (1992).

Salamon and Anheier (1997) undertake a much more comprehensive and highly useful analysis of common characteristics of non-profit organisations, which also encompass development organisations in the civil sphere. A presentation and discussion of their contribution follows in Section 5 of this chapter.

2. SOME OTHER TERMS RELATING TO DEVELOPMENT ORGANISATIONS AND THEIR PURSUITS

Students of development organisations and development work need to be acquainted with numerous terms pertaining to organisations and institutions in general, development organisations more specifically, and concerns and activities of the latter.

Some common terms of general nature are defined below. Others are defined in the following chapters, relating to topics which are addressed in those chapters.

Development institution

This is commonly considered as synonymous with 'development organisation', with the added requirement that the organisation is well known among those for whom it may be of concern and is generally recognised as serving a legitimate role in development. We may in such instances say that the organisation is 'institutionalised'.

The term 'institution' (including broader conceptions of it than just mentioned) and its relation with 'organisation' are further elaborated in Chapter Five, along with the terms 'institution-building' and 'organisation-building'.

Public institution

'Public institution' is by most analysts and users understood as any institutionalised organisation of the state and the voluntary section of the civil society. This excludes NGOs, which we, as well, have categorised as non-profit organisations within the private sphere (see Table 2.1).

Public institutions that address development may appropriately be referred to as 'public development institutions'.

In addition, certain public structures or provisions may be referred to as institutions, most notably, laws and other provisions to regulate social behaviour.

Public forum

Public forums include public organisations, but may in addition be venues or opportunities for expressions of a less clearly structured or more short-term nature. Examples of the latter may be: local community meetings, regulated demonstrations and the media.

Private institution

This is the equivalent of 'public institution' in the private sphere of societies.

In the development realm, in organised form, the term can basically be considered as synonymous with 'private non-profit (development) organisation', usually referred to as NGO or NGDO.

Development policy

This is a coherent set of general priorities of development, formulated by well institutionalised development organisations, relating to the general public or to specified groups of people, along with the kinds of measures needed to pursue development effectively according to these priorities.

Development strategy

'Strategy' is a more specific expression of intended action than 'policy'. Formulating a development strategy means to make choices about development problems to be addressed and how to address them, considering opportunities and constraints in the society as well as abilities and resources for dealing with the problems.

The concept of 'development strategy' will be further elaborated in Chapter Three.

Organisational vision

This concept, most frequently applied by NGOs and some voluntary organisations, stands for a desired future situation which the organisation (or set of organisations) intends to help create (for instance, 'a society with no maltreatment of children' or 'equal opportunities of women and men').

Organisational mission

This concept stands for the overall contribution that the organisation aims at making towards fulfilment of its vision; in other words, it expresses the very reason for its existence. An alternative term is '(organisational) purpose'.

3. INTERPRETATIONS OF THE STATE

Ideas about the state have changed substantially over time and have differed greatly between societies. The depression of the international economy around 1930 spurred an active debate about the role of the state in development. With the termination of colonial rule, a state machinery with a largely new orientation was established in the liberated countries. During the last couple of decades, there has been an intensified discussion about the state's position and performance, in both highly developed and less developed countries. In many of the latter, the discussion has partly related to forms and conditions of foreign development assistance.

Judgements about the performance of the state, in relation to development and more widely, depend, of course, on mainstream ideas at the time as well as on the political orientation and interpretations of individuals. Common contemporary points of criticism of the state are that it tends to be authoritarian, inefficient and in some instances unduly restrictive. In many developing countries, in particular, it has got an additional reputation of having many corrupt features. These problems may be broadly summed up as low responsiveness and poor accountability.

Simultaneously, the state is essential for securing basic rights of individuals and groups in complex contemporary societies and has a crucial part to play in promoting development.

There are various interpretations of the general purpose of the state and the role it should play in development. Over the next few pages, I will sum up the major ones, drawing substantially on an analysis by Maureen Mackintosh (1992).

THE PUBLIC INTEREST STATE

The public interest view of the state characterised most development thinking in the first decades after World War II, and got its manifestation in the set-up of governments and their operational systems. While this view is less predominant today, perspectives involved are still highly influential.

The government, by its politicians and civil servants, is considered capable of defining the *common interests* of the people (being frequently referred to as the 'public interest'). On this basis, government agencies should formulate policies and plans and use the powers of the state to further those interests. The government's economic advisers ought to play key roles in policy formulation. Many measures need to be implemented, as well, by agencies of the state, such as taxation, provision of a wide range of welfare services, and regulation of production.

With the words of Kliksberg (1997: 172), the state is perceived as the one institution that may 'comprehensively plan all aspects of development and implement those plans through its own machinery, carrying out those operations from the centralised level and assuming all types of executive functions'.

In short, this *top-down* model of decision-making and implementation is considered to be the most *rational* (effective and efficient) approach to development.

The state has to plan development because of perceived *market deficiencies*. The view is that the market, through interaction between supply and demand, is unable to respond to a range of needs of various groups in the society – even many needs relating to economic production.

Thus, in the economic field, the state should plan for core industries, should support other essential and promising industries financially, and may even establish state-owned enterprises.

A popular view has been that the state should plan for clusters of inter-connected industries and production units, i.e., industries and units which support each other by buying from and selling to one another. In order to exploit external economies of scale, it has often been considered advantageous to locate such entities together, in so-called growth centres.

In less developed countries, in particular, many of these industries and production units have been intended to produce commodities in replacement of imported commodities. This is referred to as import substitution.

THE CLASS-BASED STATE

This is the perspective on the state held by people influenced by the writings of Karl Marx. Besides labelling themselves 'Marxists', analysts within this broad school of thought are frequently referred to as 'structuralists' or 'dependency theorists'.

While they may have divergent views in many respects, they all agree that there exists *no common public interest*. The state is defined in relation to *social classes* and conflicts between them, and the conventional state is considered to be an institution for promoting the interests of the dominant classes.

According to orthodox Marxism, the exploiting government is destined to be overthrown, at some stage, through a revolution and replaced by a government of the masses. However, the divergence between this theory and historical realities has led many to search for more nuanced theories.

An alternative view has been that in already *industrialised countries*, the state may adjust and even promote widespread welfare, by responding to organised demand in the civil society. This may, over time, lead to reduced class differences in these countries – although conflicts of interest will persist.

In *underdeveloped countries*, however, exploiting alliances tend to be formed between the state (including the administrative service), other national elite groups, and foreign companies. The market in these countries is considered to have strong monopolistic features, consisting of units that exploit others in the interest of their owners and their allies, within and outside the country.

The state may nationalise industries. But this may just mean that the actors of the state acquire opportunities to generate more benefits for themselves. This can be done through joint ventures between state-owned companies and multinational companies, being beneficial to both parties. Foreign companies benefit from payments for patent rights, hiring out trade marks, supply of management expertise, etc. Local bureaucrats and their allies gain lucrative directorships, salaries and prestige, and may enrich themselves through misuse of public funds.

In such underdeveloped societies, class-centred theorists tend to see no alternative to a well engineered *revolution*, by which the state is made the direct representative of the deprived people.

THE PRIVATE INTEREST STATE

This is the view held by neo-liberal theorists. They disagree with both the structuralists and the public interest proponents on crucial points.

Unlike the former, they believe that competitive markets may exist and are frequently the best mechanism for allocation of resources, whereby they will also serve the interests of various groups of people.

In opposition to the public interest view, the neo-liberal theorists argue that:

- the state is not capable of objectively defining the public interest;
- the state can not be relied upon to act in a unitary manner to serve the interests of any groups, by whatever criteria the latter might be delimited.

Instead, politicians and bureaucrats will act primarily in their *own interest*, just like people who buy and sell in a market.

This does not mean that politicians and state officials are normally corrupt persons. There are still norms, rules and regulations for proper conduct, which these people are expected to obey. Nevertheless, neo-liberal theorists, as well, consider corruption to have become a serious problem, particularly in many less developed countries.

In any case, a private interest view of the state does imply that politicians and bureaucrats will tend to exploit opportunities which may exist for strengthening their own position and well-being, for strengthening the position of their bureau, and for making their day-to-day work as easy as possible. To these ends, bureaucrats emphasise such things as salaries, public reputation and patronage (protection by superiors or higher-level units).

Public bureaux have a position of *monopoly* that gives them advantages in trying to promote their own interests. By 'monopoly' is primarily meant that a bureau has access to information which others do not have, that it may be the only supplier of a service, and that it gets money from another monopoly – the Treasury. By exploiting advantages accruing from their position, the state bureau tends to grow too big. And, because it does not face direct competition, its service provision may be ineffective and costly.

Through these processes, the state becomes a 'monster', which aims at regulating activities in detail. In many instances, it is not competent to do so, and by interfering it may seriously thwart the functioning of a competitive market and even erode protective social structures.

Moreover, particularly in developing countries, expansion of the sphere of influence of the state and increased government budgets are commonly reinforced by self-aggrandisement of politicians and by alliances of various kinds between politicians and other elite groups.

Through such alliances, powerful groups of citizens, such as influential and vocal residents of major cities, may be able to acquire various state benefits for themselves. Commonly mentioned examples are cheap food (for instance, by regulations that maintain low prices to the farmers) and urban focused health and education services.

This argument of *power alliances* tends to be shared by neo-liberal and class-focusing (structuralist) critics of the state.

4. REFORMING THE STATE FOR DEVELOPMENT

The presentation in this section reflects recent lines of discussion of how the state may be made more accountable, more responsive to people's needs, and more efficient. The reader will notice that a conventional revolution alternative, based on Marxist analysis, is missing. This reflects the near-absence of such a perspective in the contemporary debate.

SCALING DOWN THE STATE

This is a basically neo-liberal reaction against what is seen as an over-ambitious, oversized and more or less poorly functioning state. The main advocated measures are:

- *Curtailing state activities*, i.e., reducing the government's expenditure in commodity production and service provision;
- *Targeting many services* to the most needy people only;
- Introducing or increasing *payment for services* by the recipients (or at least many of them).

These have been important policy measures from the early 1980s onwards, particularly in developing countries, in response to the debt crisis in many of these countries. In most cases, the measures have been largely induced by international lending and other donor organisations, for the countries to become eligible for financial assistance.

However, some Asian countries with relatively low public spending ratios earlier, such as South Korea and Indonesia, increased the state's share of investments well into the 1990s, mainly through large injections into physical infrastructure and many kinds of production enterprises.

Levying user fees, i.e., payment for services by the users, has been a main component of the structural adjustment programme of the World Bank and other international lending agencies. Such fees are intended to supplement the modest revenue which Third World governments get from general taxation. They may also reduce the demand for the services, and should make the service provision more efficient. For political and other reasons, it has in many instances proved difficult to introduce such fees and even more difficult to enforce the payment of them.

Main recommendations regarding targeting of services have been:

- if at all resorted to, subsidies on food and other basic commodities should be provided to the poorest people only;
- state-financing of higher education should be graded according to the financial ability of individual students;
- subsidised production credit should be given to clearly specified groups only, in replacement of more indiscriminate state-subsidised credit schemes, having been very common in a large number of developing countries.

Besides reducing government expenditures, some such measures have been intended to cushion the poorest people against adverse effects of other rationalisation measures.

SPLITTING AND WITHDRAWING THE STATE

Largely, these are aspects of a neo-liberal policy as well. The main measures may be specified as:

*	Deregulation	*	Devolution
*	Deconcentration	*	Privatisation
*	Delegation		

(Cheema and Rondinelli [1983]; Mackintosh [1992]).

Deregulation may basically mean:

- giving up state monopolies, particularly in commercial production of certain commodities and services which governments have reserved for public companies – such as basic industries and some kinds of transport – but even in fields such as education, provision of health services, renovation and sanitation, and water supply;

- removing or adjusting regulatory measures of investment and production which are considered to distort prices or otherwise distort or thwart the economy, such as price controls, subsidies and licensing.

The main general idea behind deregulation is to create a more competitive environment for production and service-provision, which is expected to increase efficiency.

Deregulation, in one or more of the mentioned senses, has been a common measure in most developing countries lately.

Deconcentration means redistributing certain administrative responsibilities within the central government, in particular, to lower administrative levels and regional and local offices. The main rationale is usually to make administration more efficient.

In some instances, it is considered advantageous to allocate the full responsibility for clearly specified fields of operation to such units. For instance, this may apply within departments which are intended to finance their services, in full or in part, from user fees. In such cases, substantial operational autonomy on the part of regional sub-units of these departments, being the direct providers of the services within their areas of operation, may help make those bodies more accountable to their clients, and may in addition spur them to pursue fee collection more effectively.

Examples of organisations for which this may apply are government departments in charge of water supply and certain advisory services.

By *delegation* is meant allocation of decision-making and management authority from a government body, most commonly a central government ministry, to some other organisation. Examples of organisations to which authority may be delegated are public corporations, regional development agencies, project management units, and private companies. This represents, then, a more comprehensive form of decentralisation than administrative deconcentration.

However, while the organisation to which authority is delegated will not be under direct day-to-day control by the delegating organisation, the latter (or an alternative government agency) will retain a formal role of supervision and approval at a general level, for instance, approval of annual budgets. Sometimes, the delegating agency may transfer only the implementation of activities and may even pay for or subsidise the work that is done, as is commonly the case for urban renovation, for instance.

Delegation has been a common measure adopted by governments in developing countries, in response to severe limitations of financial resources and management capability.

Devolution within government means to give bodies of government at some sub-national level or levels substantial independence from the central government, usually along with a provision for the people of the respective areas to elect their representatives to these bodies and measures to strengthen their administrative capacity. The sub-national units constitute, then, semi-independent levels of government, having jurisdiction over demarcated parts of the country. They are usually referred to as *local governments*.

The concept of 'local government' implies that the respective bodies have corporate status. This enables them to act as legally independent entities in dealings within their spheres of authority and to generate resources, independently of central government agencies, for services that they render to their constituency. Such self-acquired resources come from taxation of inhabitants of the geographical areas under their jurisdiction, in a range of forms.

In its most developed sense, such a dual system of governance implies a genuinely reciprocal relationship (relationship on basically equal legal terms) between the local governments and their nation-level counterpart (the central government) – within the legally specified framework for shared governance and within limits that are specified for preventing threats to overriding national interests.[6]

---

[6] Systems of local governance and local – central government relations vary hugely. Consequently, any analysis of local governments and devolution involves examination of a range of policy and institutional issues. A good overview of systems and contextual variables is given by Shotton (1999).

Most governments of developing countries have been reluctant to give the same amount of autonomy to local governments as has been the case in more developed countries.

The main exception is the governance of cities, which tends to be similar everywhere, due to a range of specific and complex management issues pertaining to big population agglomerations, which largely have to be taken care of by authorities of the city itself.

Local governments in rural areas – which may also include centres of different sizes – have tended to be considered as sub-units of the central government, with primary responsibility for relatively narrow and clearly specified functions only. They have also tended to be heavily dependent on the central government for financial resources, technical expertise and administrative personnel.

Moreover, even within such rather narrow confines of operation, local governments have commonly been riddled with numerous problems of day-to-day management and administration. Even more fundamental have been elite-dominance and problems of accountability to the people whom the institution is supposed to serve.

Often, therefore, most people of many less developed countries have tended not to consider the local government of their area as an institution that serves them and over which they have or may have much influence. Although elections in some form are normally held, the candidates for political positions have tended to come from narrow sections of the population only.[7]

---

[7] Except some case studies, rigorous analyses of the performance of rural local governments in developing countries are hard to come by.

A recent book edited by Aziz and Arnold (1996) seeks to synthesise much of the experience and researchers' views regarding local government in Asia, drawing on both case studies and broader country analyses.

On the whole, the book paints a rather negative and disheartening picture of the institution of local government in this continent. Simultaneously, many authors emphasise that some countries have recently passed more comprehensive local government legislation, and a few encouraging experiences are presented as well – among which I find the account of recent experiments in China particularly interesting.

Privatisation has become another major strategy for increasing the effectiveness and efficiency of both commodity production and service provision. It means transfer of ownership and operation from a government body to a private body, the latter of which will undertake the respective activities on a commercial basis (whether or not the government body ran them commercially).

There has tended to be widespread agreement over recent years that it may be desirable to privatise many production enterprises, i.e., state undertakings that governments have intended to run commercially. Often, however, privatisation has proved to be difficult to effectuate. Main reasons have been that many of these enterprises have been unprofitable and that there has been insufficient management competence elsewhere for running them in a better manner.

Privatisation òf basic government services, having been provided free of charge or at highly subsidised rates (such as education and health services), has also been deliberated and even undertaken on a limited scale in some instances. This is, usually, a politically much more contentious issue than privatisation of production enterprises. The very rationale for providing these services by the state has been to make them as readily available as possible to the whole or large sections of the population, which may no longer be possible when they are provided on a commercial basis.

A further, less direct, example of privatisation is increased recognition by the state of the role which non-governmental development organisations may play in development and, in many countries, a corresponding increase in the freedom for such organisations to access financial and other resources.

WORKING BOTTOM-UP

Those who argue for this option largely disagree with the public interest view of the state. They do not think that the state 'knows best', that it can define a common public interest, or that it can promote effectively that interest, in all its senses, through a conventional hierarchical structure and conventional bureaucratic principles of work.

They tend to agree with the structuralists that the state has primarily served privileged and influential groups. They may, simultaneously, share with the private interest school of thought the view that the state has tended to promote private rather than common interests. They may even agree with some of the reform measures prescribed by neo-liberal policy-makers.

But they do not accept the basic neo-liberal view that private interests need to be accepted as a determinant of the work that agencies of the state undertake. On the contrary: the state should seek to change its mode of work so that it can promote non-market principles of *solidarity* and become more *responsive* to the needs of deprived people, in particular.

Robert Chambers,[8] a main proponent of this view, argues that this requires a move away from 'normal professionalism', which promotes conventional bureaucratic organisation and modes of work, cements centralisation and standardisation, and provides simplified solutions.

Work of standardised and repetitive nature may be performed well by a conventional state bureaucracy, even when undertaken on a big scale. Examples may be nation-wide primary education, vaccination campaigns, and many kinds of engineering works. But the normal bureaucracy is ill-equipped to respond to diverse and varying needs and complex and changing situations. Consequently, it tends to undertake much development work of multifaceted nature poorly, particularly if it is also done in changing environments. Thus, says Chambers, this bureaucracy, with its top-down approach and its standardised procedures and solutions, can hardly be expected to promote rural development effectively.

According to Chambers, rural development work ought to emphasise the position and living condition of poor and otherwise deprived people, being strongly influenced by their diverse environments. Consequently, such work needs to be based on good information about the specific factors that influence the people's

---

[8] See, in particular, Chambers (1993).

lives and must be flexible enough for diverse and complex problems to be addressed through diverse and changing measures. This requires a *process* mode of work and active *learning*. It also calls for *decentralisation* within government and active *participation* by people in problem analysis and decision-making.

Fulfilment of these basic requirements necessitates, in turn, a range of measures, such as:

- higher status of and rewards for field staff;
- accepting failures and shortcomings as lessons for the future more than as causes for punishment;
- information and control systems which allow and encourage interaction with service users;
- greater local control over resources.

Over the last 10 to 15 years, such thoughts have been sought to be incorporated into some government-run rural development programmes in some countries. One problem has been that the new ideas have tended to be promoted more by donor staff or consultants than by the country's own politicians and administrators. Another hindering factor has been difficulties in adjusting the financial systems of both the national governments and the donor agencies for greater flexibility of operation, being a condition for operationalising a bottom-up approach.

FACILITATIVE GOVERNANCE

The concept of 'facilitative governance', as used here, covers a broad and more or less inter-linked set of ideas about the desired role and modes of work of state institutions in development.

A basic tenet is that the 'public interest' state is too rigid and imposing, preventing it from performing an enabling or facilitative role vis-à-vis other societal institutions. However, scaling down and withdrawing the state is hardly the answer, because a 'minimalist' state may come to lack both the authority and the management ability to facilitate development.

The perceived need for facilitative governance is underpinned by a recognition of increasing *societal complexity* all over the world, the basic driving force of which is technological advancement on many fronts. One major consequence of this is increasing economic and social inequality and a concomitant *marginalisation* of large numbers of people, particularly in economically less developed countries. The latter also reflects a third characterising feature: increasing complexity and diversity go along with, and are conditioned by, stronger and more complex patterns of *interdependency* – between production enterprises, between societies, and between population groups within countries and regions.

In this setting, the state is perceived to have a crucial role to play in mediating the market forces and counteracting marginalisation. In addition to *regulatory* measures of the market, the state should devise and employ mechanisms for *facilitating* economic and social life, it should itself be *directly in charge* of basic social services for the population at large and additional measures for vulnerable groups, and it should actively *promote civil society organisations* to be formed and address numerous issues of welfare and development.

A particularly important concern is to combat a common notion of the state as being an 'enemy of civil society' (Kliksberg [1997]). If they get recognition, encouragement and adequate operating space by the government, organisations of the civil society have a commonly underestimated ability to address social problems – by promoting desirable values and social responsibility, by strengthening social networks of many kinds, by activating people, and through engagement in more specific activities, such as adult education and vocational training.

For many purposes, civil institutions may even be made officially recognised partners of government bodies, on a flexible basis, depending on opportunities at any time.

This perspective is related to the notion of 'strategic management', developed primarily in the business world, in that it requires continuous 'scanning' of opportunities and constraints in the society and, concomitantly, substantial flexibility of operation. We may, therefore, alternatively refer to this perspective of the state as 'strategic governance'.[9] The perspective is also interfaced with that of working 'bottom-up', just addressed.

We may also relate this view to certain models of managing government presented by Mintzberg (1996). He distinguishes between: government as machine, government as network, performance control, virtual-government, and normative control. Effective and efficient governments may need to apply some blend of all of them. However, in Mintzberg's view, we should be more appreciative than we have normally been of the network model (although it may be easily misused as well) and 'we sorely need a major shift of emphasis to the normative model' (1996: 82). Together, these two models encompass much of what we have emphasised here.

Working in a facilitative and flexible mode may require a range of organisational reforms. Prime among them may be: developing an attitude of co-operation (rather than domain defence); deconcentration and devolution (addressed a few pages back); and application of 'soft' mechanisms of co-ordination, such as promoting a common vision, promoting common objectives, and mutual adjustment (to be elaborated in the last section of Chapter Four).

5. AN ELABORATION OF NON-PROFIT ORGANISATIONS

In Section 1, I made a distinction between two main kinds of non-profit organisations, namely, member organisations and service organisations, being located in the voluntary sector and the private sector respectively. I also clarified that the concepts of 'member –' and 'service organisation' largely correspond to those of 'mutual benefit –' and 'public benefit organisation'.

Based on a thorough examination of non-profit organisations in many countries, Salamon and Anheier (1997) provide a comprehen-

---

[9]   For an elaboration of 'strategy' and related concepts in the development field, see Chapter Three.

sive definition, with international applicability, of what they refer to as the non-profit sector. Their definition applies to the whole range of non-profit organisations of the civil society (extending far beyond the sphere of development organisations). That, however, does not make the definition less applicable for organisations in the development field.

Before arriving at their definition, Salamon and Anheier consider four categories of definitions of non-profit organisations, based on different criteria: the legal, the economic/financial, the functional, and the structural-operational definition. These are the main types of definitions applied in various national and international classifications of organisations.

Legally defined non-profit organisations are those that are specified in the laws of a country as non-profit entities. The main reason for such a classification is usually to enable the non-profit bodies to be exempted from taxation.

The legal definition of some countries covers a broad range of non-profit organisations. However, the definition differs substantially between countries. In a few countries, non-profit organisations are not even recognised in the national laws. For these reasons, a legal definition is virtually useless for analysis at the international level.

The *economic/financial* definition delimits non-profit organisations by their sources of income. In order to qualify under this criterion, the organisations must get at least most of their income from dues and contributions from their members or supporters. Organisations that receive all or most of their income from fees or charges for services rendered or as grants from governments will not be categorised as non-profit entities.

This unduly restricts the number of organisations of a society that are considered to have a voluntary or non-profit service base. For development organisations, the restriction vis-à-vis government grants is particularly unreasonable.

The *functional* definition classifies organisations according to their overall purpose. Organisations that pursue matters of public interest or create benefits for their members without generating profit may then be categorised as non-profit organisations. To the extent that single organisations emphasise one of the two (which is usually the case), this basically corresponds to our distinction between public benefit and mutual benefit organisations.

While this distinction between public and mutual interests or benefits is of great significance in many respects, it is highly problematic to define types of organisations by their assumed public benefit. That is both because non-profit organisations are not the only type of organisations that address public interests, and because what is considered as public interest varies substantially between societies and may also change over time.

The *structural-operational* definition emphasises basic structural features and modes of operation of the organisations. Salamon and Anheier consider a definition of non-profit organisations by such structural and operational characteristics to be far more appropriate than defining them by any of the other criteria.

Five structural and operational characteristics are considered by these authors to be most compelling. The non-profit sector is, thus, defined as a collection of entities that are:

- *organised*: being recognised in their environment as units of their own; having a clearly recognisable structure, regular meetings, and rules of procedure; and lasting over a substantial period of time;
- *private*: being institutionally separate from the government;
- *non-profit-distributing*: not returning any profits generated to their owners or directors;
- *self-governing*: not being subject to substantial control by another body or other bodies, and having their internal procedures of governance;
- *voluntary*: involving 'some meaningful degree of voluntary participation, either in the conduct of the organisation's activities or in the management of its affairs'.

Salamon and Anheier's analysis demonstrates convincingly that a definition of non-profit organisations by such structural and operational criteria is the most appropriate one. For purposes of comparison, nationally and even more internationally, it may even be the only useful definition. Also, the set of structural and operational features that Salamon and Anheier emphasise appear to be basically appropriate.

However, I have a comment relating to the dimensions of 'private' and 'voluntary' in Salamon and Anheier's framework.

In my view, one should recognise more clearly the basic distinction between *mutual benefit* organisations and *public benefit* organisations, which I have made above and which these authors refer to as well. This basically reflects the distinction made in this chapter between *voluntary* organisations and *private* organisations.

Going by common notions about benevolent organisations, it may seem logical to argue, as Salamon and Anheier do, that voluntarism should be present to at least some extent in all organisations of non-profit nature. Usually, however, this is a prime characterising feature of member organisations, while it may be hard to trace in many service organisations. I think that Salamon and Anheier's own elaboration on voluntarism, that 'the presence of some voluntary input, even if only a voluntary board of directors, suffices ...', underlines my argument.

The point is, then, to ensure that all non-profit organisations are unambiguously incorporated under the definition of the non-profit sector, including private organisations with very limited or even no readily traceable voluntary features.

This modification may be taken care of by slight modifications of the set of structural and operational characteristics specified by Salamon and Anheier, namely, by replacing the word 'private' (the second characteristic in the list on the previous page) with 'voluntary or private' and by deleting the separate criterion of 'voluntary' (the last-mentioned in the list).

Additionally, with reference to the presentation in Section 2 of this chapter and the further analysis that will be undertaken in

Chapter Five, I prefer to refer to organisational entities as 'inst-itutionalised' rather than just 'organised', for them to be conceived of as development organisations.

In summary, then, and in supplement of the typology presented in the first section of this Chapter, I consider *non-profit development organisations* within the civil sphere to be entities that are:

- *institutionalised*
- *voluntary or private*
- *not profit-distributing*
- *self-governing.*

6. ROLES AND PERFORMANCE OF NON-GOVERNMENTAL DEVELOPMENT ORGANISATIONS

The term 'non-governmental organisation' ('NGO') is here used synonymously with 'non-profit service organisation'. In Section 1, this was stated to be the most common usage of the term NGO. By adding the word 'development' – by which we get 'non-govern-mental development organisation' ('NGDO') – we have unambigu-ously delimited our field of concern to service organisations in the realm of societal development.

Both member organisations and private service organisations perform a wide range of development roles. However, member organisations with a mutual benefit mission (being the normal com-bination) have a much more unified purpose than service organisa-tions, namely, augmenting their members' benefits, in some sense, through joint organisation and action. By their character of support or service providers for others (whether these are direct beneficiar-ies or other development organisations), NGDOs commonly have to address a wider range of strategic issues and to consider a wider spectrum of strategic choices.[10] Consequently, their overall purpose

---

[10] The concepts of 'strategy' and 'strategic choice' in a development context are defined and discussed in Chapter Three.

varies greatly and they perform highly diverse roles in development of the societies in which they operate.

Main *purposes* (*missions*) of different kinds of NGDOs are indicated below:

Relief work

The focus is here on the survival and immediate care of people in various emergency situations, such as wars and natural calamities.[11]

Provision of welfare services

Main examples of welfare services provided by NGDOs are: preschools for children, primary education, adult education, water supply and sanitation, health education, and health care.

Provision of production-related services

This may involve experiments of various kinds (such as trials of crops or cultivation techniques); advise or training in technology, organisation or management; financial services; or promotion of technical innovations.

Promotion of local self-reliant development

This encompasses efforts to build new or support existing community institutions as well as to augment the ability of disadvantaged individuals and households to cope better with forces that influence their lives. The latter is commonly referred to as empowerment.[12]

Building national and sub-national institutions

Various kinds of support may be rendered to government institutions, such as promoting or improving public laws and regulations, policy advice, and improving the operational performance of state

---

[11]   Some would not consider relief work as development work and would therewith not label organisations that focus wholly or mainly on such work as NGDOs. I consider this to be a highly questionable restriction, both conceptually and due to problems of delimitation. See also footnote no. 2 of this chapter.

[12]   For definition and further discussion of 'empowerment', see Chapter Five.

organisations. Also, NGDOs may strengthen the capability of civil organisations, particularly smaller NGDOs and voluntary organisations (also other than those confined to local communities, just mentioned) and help institutionalise them as effective development agents.[13]

Advocacy

This means to augment awareness and to build attitudes among the public (at the international, national or local level) relating to some social problem, basic rights of groups of people, means of obtaining such rights, etc.

One author (Korten [1987]) has suggested that development focusing NGOs tend to move through stages of purpose or so-called generations. The first-generation NGOs focus on relief and welfare, the second-generation ones emphasise local self-reliance through organisation and mobilisation of local resources, and the third-generation ones move on to challenge policies and institutions at national and sub-national levels.

While certain tendencies in this direction may have been discernible in the 1980s, the general linear progression suggested by the author is questionable. In fact, a concern has recently been raised by some authors about a perceived tendency over later years to concentrate more on welfare services, in particular, in response to increased donor support to NGDOs for such work.[14]

NGDOs have played major *roles* in all the above mentioned fields. Moreover, in a majority of countries, the part played by NGDOs in development has certainly been increasing.

Simultaneously, in view of the great diversity of NGDOs and the environment in which they work, it goes virtually without saying that the *performance* of NGDOs has been very diverse as well. This

---

[13]   The concepts of 'institution' and 'institution-building' are further clarified in Chapter Five.

[14]   See, for instance, Biggs and Neame (1996) and other contributions in Edwards and Hulme (1996).

is not the place to delve into an examination of the quality of work of various kinds of NGDOs operating under widely different conditions. Brief references to main conclusions by a few analysts will have to suffice.

The following passages from Edwards and Hulme (1996) underline some of the diversity and the complexities involved:

> There is increasing evidence that NGOs ... do not perform as effectively as has been assumed in terms of poverty reach, cost-effectiveness, sustainability, popular participation (including gender), flexibility and innovation. In terms of service provision, there is certainly evidence that NGOs are able to provide some services more cost-effectively than governments. ... However, ... there is no empirical study that demonstrates a general case that NGO provision is cheaper than public provision. Even when NGO service provision is low-cost, it usually fails to reach the poorest people, though it may still reach a wider cross-section of the population than government or commercial agencies. The sustainability of large-scale service provision by NGOs has also been called into question. ... In all cases, careful management is needed to avoid a falloff in quality when NGOs scale up service provision to cover large populations... (1996: 5).

> Evidence on the performance of NGOs ... in democratization is more difficult to come by, except in the area of micropolicy reform, where a growing number of case studies demonstrate that NGOs ... can influence governments and official agencies ... . [However, in many places] NGOs have had little impact on political reform, partly because states are adept at containing such a possibility, and partly because NGOs themselves have failed to develop effective strategies to promote democratization (1996: 5-6).

> [This] is not to claim that NGOs perform less effectively than other organizations ... , but simply to point out that they often perform less well than their popular image suggests. ... There is reason to believe that any differences that do emerge have less to do with inherent traits and more to do with factors that cut across the public-private divide (1996: 7).

Others consider the performance of NGOs, in general, to have been more clearly positive and emphasise more comparative advantages which they think they have. Thus, with particular reference to rural development, Chambers (1993) emphasises three fields in which NGOs have shown to have advantages over government agencies. These are:

- working with people in a process mode: to start small, be sensitive, question, learn, adapt, and improve gradually;

- developing new methods of analysis (such as rapid and participatory rural appraisal);

- developing new institutions at the local level, notably, strong people's organisations and village development catalysts.

Chambers thinks that it is important for NGOs to work on a small scale until they, through processes of learning, have 'got things right'. Then they may be capable to expand, to share experiences, and even to teach others.

Since good NGOs have this ability to learn, to develop alternative methods of work, and to work with others, Chambers is of the view that more NGOs should make training (also of government agencies) a more important part of their work.

However, Chambers (1996) is also concerned about a tendency, perceived by him, of NGOs becoming more bureaucratic and top-down orientated. This occurs largely in response to greater financial dependence on international donor agencies, which themselves work in such modes and require the same of the organisations that receive their support. Consequently, the NGOs come under pressure to formulate projects quickly for approval, apply rigid and simple planning tools, and disburse money fast.

The composition, role and performance of NGOs in any country depends on many factors, of both location-specific and more general nature. Green and Matthias (1995) sum up the major ones as:

- *historical factors*: the country's history of political and economic development and the role which NGOs have performed in the past;

- *resource factors*: the particular resource constraints facing a country's government, in terms of finances, manpower, foreign exchange, etc.;
- *national ideological factors*: the political ideology of the country's rulers, directly influencing the government's attitude to NGOs;
- *international ideology*: the current beliefs and policies of the major international development agencies.

Obviously, a determinant of the role of NGDOs in any country is the *relationship between the government and the NGO sector*. This has ranged from hostility through indifference to co-operation, reflecting the above mentioned factors as well as more specific attitudes by NGOs themselves.

Referring to such different sentiments and positions, Thomas (1992), referring to Clarke (1991),[15] suggests that NGDOs may basically pursue one of the following three strategies (1992: 140):

Complementing the state

Filling in gaps, by providing services that they are better equipped to provide than the state, or by providing jointly with the state a variety of services in response to a variety of needs among the population;

Opposing the state

Working against attitudes or actions of the state, either directly by lobbying on national or international arenas, or indirectly by supporting local and national groups that are adversely affected by government policies;

Reforming the state

Representing the interests of disadvantaged groups at the level of government or working with the government to improve policies of the latter.

---

[15] Clarke, J. (1991): *Democratizing Development: the role of voluntary organisations;* London: Earthscan.

Examining relations between governmental organisations (GOs) and NGOs in agricultural development in Asia, Farrington and Lewis (1993) identify the following main sets of partnerships and the roles that NGOs have in these (1993: 301–14):

1. 'NGO-GO partnerships within the research-extension continuum', in which NGOs play the role of field testers of technologies developed in government organisations and field centres;

2. 'NGO-GO partnerships independent of the research-extension continuum', in which NGOs are employed by the government to organise and possibly train local groups for adopting available technology;

3. 'NGOs innovate; GO response varies', involving the expectation of NGOs that their innovations (regarding technology, management practices, research methods, etc.) will be 'scaled up' by the government through its more comprehensive extension network – meeting with different degrees of interest and ability by the government;

4. 'NGOs as networkers among themselves and with GOs'; i.e., establishment of forums of NGOs for discussing common matters, and forums in which NGOs and GOs may address issues of common interest and modes of co-operation, in order to realise anticipated benefits for the organisations themselves and for their intended beneficiaries;

5. 'NGOs advocate; GO response varies'; i.e., NGOs seeking legislative or administrative reform or proper implementation of existing laws and procedures, for fulfilling the needs and securing the interests of disadvantaged groups – meeting with varying responses by the government.

The authors conclude that attempts to work as partners have most often met with substantial obstacles and that the results of co-operative endeavours have tended to be below expectations. However, variations are big, between countries as well as between the partnership categories just mentioned.

In highly general terms,

- *on 1.*, GO researchers have failed to heed the NGOs' call for bringing farmers' views into the research agenda, due to emphasis on different beneficiary groups, different modes of administration and management, and limited commitment by the majority of GO staff;
- *on 2.*, examples are found of good partnerships, but the arrangements tend to overload NGOs with rather narrow operational tasks, detracting from more normative concerns;
- *on 3.*, some cases of scaling up by GOs have been documented, while in most cases expectations have remained unfulfilled, because of differences of perception, problems of generalising from individual cases, and bureaucratic requirements on the part of the government;
- *on 4.*, intensive interaction among NGOs has been exceptional, while examples of co-operation between GOs and NGOs are documented in a few single projects;
- *on 5.*, the little documentation that has been produced reveals generally poor response by governments and strong restrictions against changes on the government side.

How can NGOs best augment their development role and increase the effectiveness and impacts of their efforts? Edwards and Hulme (1992) propose a simple yet constructive framework for analysing much of this, under the concept of 'scaling-up'. They distinguish between the following main strategic choices:

- *additive* strategies, implying an increase in the size of the respective organisation or programme;
- *multiplicative* strategies, which do not imply growth of the inducing programme or organisation, but aim at enhancing impacts by systematically influencing others through networking or training or by pursuing policy – or legal reform;
- *diffusive* strategies, by which influence and impacts are promoted in more informal and spontaneous ways.

The best strategy or blend of strategies will, obviously, depend on numerous factors, and will usually require that the NGOs explore strengths, weaknesses, opportunities, constraints and threats frequently and systematically.[16]

Of course, such strategies of scaling-up are additional measures to efforts, commonly of a current nature, that organisations may need to make in order to increase the effectiveness and impacts of their endeavours, within the limits of existing organisational entities and ongoing programmes and projects.

In this chapter, we have developed a typology of development organisations, explored main features and roles of the most important types, and reflected on issues of performance. We shall now turn our attention to how these organisations conceptualise and plan their development pursuits, under the broad heading of 'strategy formulation'. In the process, we shall discuss several notions and facets of strategic planning, link the concept to main categories of development endeavours (programmes and projects), and explore means-ends relations in development work.

---

[16] These concepts, relating to strategic planning, will be briefly examined in Chapter Three.

Chapter Three

STRATEGY FORMULATION FOR DEVELOPMENT

1. DEVELOPMENT STRATEGY, STRATEGY FORMULATION AND STRATEGIC PLANNING

The term 'strategy' tends to be used with numerous shades of meaning, in different contexts and by different authors. For initial clarification, I will broadly define the <u>strategy</u> of an organisation as the *mediating force between the organisation and its environment.* That is, it expresses how the organisation relates to its surroundings (environment) for achieving something that it aims at.[1]

Our concern are strategies of development organisations (as defined in Chapter Two), pertaining to all their pursuits or to individual programmes or projects.

Development organisations are created to address some *problem* in their environment. Moreover, they are, normally, characterised by an explicit focus on problems that affect specified groups of *people.* In the case of mutual benefit organisations, these people will be the organisations' members. For public benefit organisations, they will be outsiders.

---

[1] This conception of 'strategy' is shared by many authors. The formulation in italics is borrowed from Mintzberg (1983: 13).

By implication, the work of development organisations must be judged primarily by its influence on some aspect of the living situation of the intended beneficiaries.[2]

Moreover, I will argue that the core feature of development work is that it emphasises aspects of poverty and deprivation, as was discussed in Chapter One. Genuine development organisations will, therefore, incorporate poor or deprived people (in absolute or more relative senses) as beneficiaries of their pursuits and may even focus exclusively on less advantaged sections of the population in the societies where they work.

The above stated concerns should, then, be embedded in the concept of <u>development strategy</u>, being a commonly used term for expressing thrusts of development-focusing organisations.

In devising a strategy for dealing with the identified problem, the organisation specifies *objectives* for the intended work and identifies the types and magnitude of *outputs* that are required for fulfilling the objectives. Further, the organisation mobilises *resources* (financial capital, physical capital and personnel), which will be converted into inputs for the activities that are intended to be carried out, and it tries to fit the objectives and resources with organisational *abilities*, as envisaged during implementation. If the planning organisation intends to implement the work itself, these will be its own abilities; if some other organisation is to do the work, it will be the abilities of that body. These abilities are the combined effects of the policies and principles of work (rules) that the organisation intends to follow; the technology that it has or may acquire or develop; and its form, culture, systems of administration and rewards (incentives).[3]

---

[2]   Using common concepts in development planning, one should be able to relate the outputs (the direct outcome) of the work that is done (which may be of material or non-material nature) to effects and impacts of these outputs for intended beneficiaries. These concepts will be further elaborated later in the chapter.

[3]   These terms will be defined and discussed further in Chapter Four.

Moreover, in formulating a strategy, the organisation needs to analyse *opportunities* as well as *constraints* and *threats* in its environment (or in the environment of any other involved organisations) relating to the work that is to be done. Such opportunities, constraints and threats will, of course, influence the feasibility of addressing problems and how one should deal with them. The organisation should endeavour to eliminate or reduce current constraints, and it should carefully assess the likelihood of being confronted with additional future constraints – threats – and, as far as possible, devise means to counteract them. Conversely, it should seek to exploit optimally opportunities for fulfilling the objectives that may currently exist or may be envisaged in the future.

In summary, <u>strategy formulation</u> by a development organisation involves *identifying people-connected problems, making choices about the problem or problems to be addressed, and deciding on objectives and general courses of action – considering opportunities, constraints and threats in the environment of the involved organisation or organisations, available resources, and organisational abilities.*

As thus conceived, 'strategy' is a planning-connected concept, i.e., the above mentioned aspects will be addressed in the planning of work that organisations intend to undertake.[4] Any strategy analysis that contributes to a plan for work to be done may, therefore, be referred to as <u>strategic planning</u> or, in the development realm, <u>strategic development planning</u>.

In the sphere of development, there are also other terms that are used more or less synonymously with 'strategic (development) planning'. Among the most common ones are 'framework planning' and

---

[4] One also sees the term 'strategy' used with a broader and less specific meaning, similar to 'approach'. It is sometimes even used in relation to other functions (main work categories) in development work than planning, e.g., in the combination 'implementation strategy'. I recommend that the word 'strategy' be avoided in such connections. One may instead use formulations such as 'implementation approach' or 'mode of implementation'. For further elaboration on other work categories than planning, see Chapter Four.

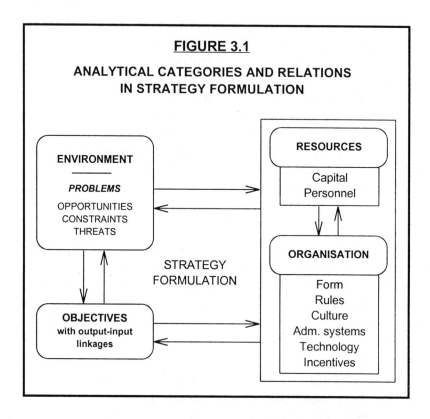

FIGURE 3.1

ANALYTICAL CATEGORIES AND RELATIONS IN STRATEGY FORMULATION

ENVIRONMENT

PROBLEMS

OPPORTUNITIES
CONSTRAINTS
THREATS

OBJECTIVES
with output-input
linkages

STRATEGY
FORMULATION

RESOURCES

Capital
Personnel

ORGANISATION

Form
Rules
Culture
Adm. systems
Technology
Incentives

'overall planning', both of which tell that the issues addressed in such planning are of relatively *basic* and *general* nature.[5]

The main concepts of and relations in strategy formulation, directly applicable for development organisations, are illustrated in Figure 3.1.

As mentioned, a strategy that a development organisation works out may pertain to its entire pursuit or to parts of it (i.e., to its whole portfolio of activities, to one type of work, or to one programme or project). The scope and focus will, obviously, influence how detailed the strategy analysis will be.

---

[5]　More detailed planning is commonly referred to as 'operational planning'. I will briefly address this later in the chapter.

The two terms 'strategy formulation' and 'strategic planning' may be used largely interchangeably. However, I suggest that one considers the former as most appropriate for clarifying the general thrust of development organisations, and the latter as the best term in relation to more specific pursuits, i.e., development programmes and projects.

The strategy of a development organisation – whether all-encompassing or partial – may be seen as embedded in an even broader conceptual frame of the intended development work, also encompassing what we in Chapter Two (Section 2) referred to as the organisation's *vision* and *mission*.

2. PLANNING MODES

We can specify numerous <u>dimensions</u> of strategic planning, by different criteria. I will here identify and briefly elaborate a set of dimensions that will, to various extents, have to be addressed in virtually any strategic planning exercise relating to development work, whether this is done explicitly or more implicitly. Each of these dimensions may be perceived as constituting a continuum between a pair of opposite 'pure' categories or forms of planning, which I will refer to as 'planning modes'.[6]

These pairs of <u>planning modes</u> may be conceptualised and termed as follows:

Normative	—	*Functional*
Comprehensive	—	*Selective*
Integrated	—	*Disjointed*
Blueprint	—	*Process*
From above	—	*From below*
Excluding	—	*Participatory*

[6] The concept of planning mode, in this sense, was initially developed by Andreas Faludi. Among his publications, see, in particular, Faludi 1973a and 1973b.

Thus, each set of modes, in 'pure' form, expresses the two end-points of one dimension of planning.[7]

These dimensions address the scope of planning (what to do, where and for whom to work), its time dimensions, its degree of flexibility, and the kinds of actors involved.

The dimensions of planning, expressed by their pairs of opposite planning modes, will be briefly elaborated in the following couple of pages.

Thereafter, we will connect the sets of modes to our framework of strategy formulation in the preceding section, and we will subsequently in the book refer to such modes in various contexts.

Normative – Functional

Any development organisation will have aims (objectives) for its work. Some development programmes and projects may have high-level development aims incorporated in them (for instance, 'improved position of women' in a county or among a population group or 'improved nutritional status of children' in a district), and the responsible organisation may not want to consider the programme or project to have been successfully completed until it has verified that these high-level aims have been fulfilled to a significant extent. Such programmes and projects may be termed highly normative and the planning organisation may be said to plan in a normative mode.

In other programmes and projects, the planning organisation may be concerned with more specific aims only, at lower levels of means-ends chains of development (for instance, 'improved school buildings' in an area or 'higher vocational skills' of groups of young people) and may be satisfied once it has verified that these aims have been attained. Such programmes and projects will have a more functional perspective and the planning organisation may be said to plan in a more functional mode.

---

[7] This set of dimensions and modes is more diverse and more specific than Faludi's framework.

Comprehensive – Selective

This dimension signifies the breadth of a development programme or project, i.e., whether it addresses only one, a few or many development issues relating to one, a few or many population groups. A selective scheme addresses only one or, at most, few issues and may focus on people defined by very specific criteria only. A comprehensive scheme addresses many issues, often for diverse population groups.

Integrated – Disjointed

The components of a development scheme – such as different activities or outputs – may be connected to each other, to larger or lesser extents, or they may be unconnected. Components which are connected to one another are commonly referred to as complementary or integrated. The dimension of 'integrated – disjointed' denotes the magnitude and strength of relations (i.e., the degree of complementarity) between the components of a development scheme: the more its components are connected to each other, the more integrated is the scheme.

This dimension is primarily of relevance for programmes. As will be clarified in Section 5, projects, by definition, consist of interconnected activities and outputs – although the links may be of different strength.

Blueprint – Process

Blueprint planning basically means that one prepares detailed plans for all that one intends to do before implementing any of that work, so that the implementers know exactly what they are to do in which sequence until the development scheme is completed. Process planning means that plans are not finalised or specified fully prior to the start-up of implementation; that is, a greater or lesser amount of planning is done in the course of the implementation period of the scheme, interactively with implementation and monitoring.[8]

---

[8] For definitions of 'implementation' and 'monitoring', see Chapter Four.

The elaboration of programmes and projects in Section 5 will clarify that projects should always be conceived of as entities planned in the blueprint mode. The concept of process planning is, therefore, applicable to programmes only. An exception may be when one plans a project in stages, utilising experiences from the implementation of previous stages in the planning of subsequent stages. However, in many such instances, one may refer to such a development endeavour as a programme with several projects (rather than a project of several stages).

In any strategic planning exercise of a development scheme, one must know or clarify whether that exercise is the only strategic planning event for that scheme or whether it is one of more such events. In the former case, one plans strategically for a programme that is to be further specified through blueprint planning, before the implementation of it starts, or for a project (which will always be of blueprint nature). In the latter case, one plans strategically for a programme of process nature; i.e., one will or may – within limits – expand, contract or adjust the programme or parts of it during subsequent strategic planning events.

From above – From below

The issue here is who are involved in problem identification, idea generation and decision-making, by level in the respective society or organisation. The more influence that is exerted by beneficiaries or other persons at the field level or by lower-level staff in the organisation, the more from below is the planning; the more the purpose and activities are decided on by people at top levels, the more from above is the planning.

A much used alternative set of terms is 'top-down – bottom-up'.

Excluding – Participatory

This denotes the number and variety of individuals and/or organisational units that are involved in the various stages of planning, at whichever level in the respective society or organisation. Excluding planning is done by key professionals in a directly responsible agency only, whereas participatory planning will involve more people who may have an interest in or may be affected by the intended programme or project.

We may refer to these dimensions by their pair names; i.e., we may talk of the 'normative – functional dimension', the 'blueprint – process dimension', etc. We could also give each dimension a separate name. For instance, we might refer to the 'from above – from below dimension' as the 'direction of planning' or something similar, and the 'normative – functional dimension' as the 'value scope in planning' or simply the 'value dimension'.

We can now consolidate this discussion by linking these planning categories to our initial basic framework, presented in Section 1 and visually summarised in Figure 3.1. We then see that the first three dimensions (normative – functional, comprehensive – selective, integrated – disjointed) express various aspects of what we may refer to as the objectives-environment-resources nexus (i.e., the kinds of problems addressed and the coverage and composition of activities, being closely related to the available resources). The last three dimensions (blueprint – process, from above – from below, excluding – participatory) are, most directly, expressions of rules of work, broadly conceptualised.

Simultaneously, all the above may be influenced by and exert influence on other variables incorporated in the figure, such as various other aspects of organisation. Consequently, such other aspects, as well, may need to be considered in strategic planning. However, detailed analysis of organisational aspects, along with specification of outputs, resource issues, etc., are mainly undertaken in subsequent operational planning.

Thus, in conclusion, our set of planning modes encompasses the variables of our strategy model that are addressed *primarily* in strategic planning; they do not embed variables that may need to be *generally considered* in strategic planning but are primarily analysed in subsequent operational planning (see also Section 4 of the present chapter).

I have defined 'dimension of planning' as a *continuum* between opposite extreme or 'pure' categories (modes). Real-world planning hardly ever manifests any set of modes in their pure form, and should not be interpreted or described as such. One should, instead, talk of degrees of application of any mode.

For instance, a development programme may be characterised by highly normative features, a certain combination of blueprint and process planning, some participation in certain activities by some categories of people, etc.

The notion of dimension continuum may be visualised by a line connecting the imaginary endpoints on the dimension under study, each of which represents opposite planning modes in their extreme form. The actual mode of planning within any programme or project may then be specified by locating it somewhere on this line, as exemplified in Figure 3.2. Among the cases in the figure, project A practices planning most from above and project C practices planning most from below.

We need a lot of information about the workings of a programme or project to be able to judge, reasonably reliably, where on such a continuum it belongs.

By locating a programme or project on all the planning dimensions, i.e., by specifying the combination of planning modes for the particular scheme, we get what we may call the *strategy configuration* of that programme or project.

Moreover, by analysing choices of strategy, we find that some planning modes tend to fit well together while others do not. For instance, planning largely 'from below' will commonly require substantial 'process' orientation, and 'normative' planning may require a 'comprehensive' perspective.

Such exercises may be helpful for exploring relations between performance and achievements on the one hand and aspects of planning on the other. They may be particularly useful in comparative evaluative studies of similar programmes and projects, in tracing how planning may have influenced subsequent adherence to plans, work efficiency and benefits. The issue is, then, whether and how differences in modes of planning and different combinations of such

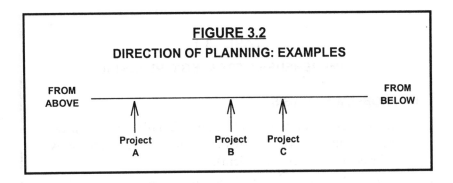

FIGURE 3.2
DIRECTION OF PLANNING: EXAMPLES

modes may help explain differences of relevance, efficiency, effectiveness, impacts and even sustainability of the programme or project which is evaluated.[9]

3. STEPS, LINKS AND ISSUES IN COMPREHENSIVE STRATEGIC PLANNING

In strategic planning, the emphasis that will be placed on different dimensions and issues and the depth and thoroughness of analysis will vary greatly. Any exercise will depend on or be influenced by numerous factors, such as: the type, magnitude, complexity and uncertainty of the development endeavour; the kind and number of organisations involved; the degrees of freedom which the organisations have; the capability of the planners; and the set of external interest groups (stakeholders).

In Table 3.1, an outline is given of main aspects that commonly have to be addressed in strategic planning. The table should be seen as a check-list of variables, linkages and issues. Thorough analysis of all of them may be needed in rare instances only.

---

[9] For an empirical analysis of strategy configurations in rural development programmes and relations between planning modes and programme achievements, see Dale (1992).

For definition and elaboration of the mentioned concepts of evaluation, see Chapter Six.

TABLE 3.1

COMPREHENSIVE STRATEGIC PLANNING

1. PROBLEM ANALYSIS

- Make a statement of the problem which most clearly expresses the difficulty experienced by the people affected (commonly referred to as the core problem);
- Identify direct causes and, if appropriate, direct effects of the core problem;
- Identify further cause-effect links, resulting in a more or less complex cause-effect diagram (often referred to as a problem tree).

2. ANALYSIS OF EXTERNAL STAKEHOLDERS

- Identify the stakeholders by their stakes:
  * those who are affected by the problem
  * those who cause the problem
  * those who may be affected by measures against the problem
  * those who may contribute in dealing with the problem
  * those who may work against envisaged measures
  * any other organisation, programme or project which may undertake similar measures as envisaged, partly or fully;
- Categorise the stakeholders by type of unit (individuals, interest groups, private organisations, government agencies, etc.);
- Get an overview of the needs and interests of each category of stakeholders;
- Discuss and decide on whose needs, interests and views should be given priority;
- Analyse further the needs and interests of the prioritised individuals, groups or organisations and clarify in greater detail who should be beneficiaries;

- Analyse the strengths and weaknesses of potential external contributors, i.e., individuals, groups and organisations which may be involved in or otherwise contribute to the envisaged work;
- Analyse the strength of the threats posed by any hostile individuals, groups and organisations.

⇒ *Feedback to the problem analysis (1)*

3. FORMULATION OF OBJECTIVES WITH LINKAGES

- Reformulate the cause-effect diagram (1) into positive statements, i.e., into desirable achievements (objectives) and underlying requirements of these (types of outputs and inputs);
- Discuss and decide on any revision, deletion or addition of objectives, in the light of:
  * the legitimacy and importance of any objections by any stakeholders to intended measures;
  * whether or to what extent any objectives may be fulfilled by development work that is being or may be undertaken by others.

⇒ *Feedback to the stakeholder analysis (particularly, decision on beneficiaries) (2)*

4. ASSESSMENT OF RESOURCES

- Estimate broadly the requirement for money, equipment and personnel (with adequate abilities) for attaining the envisaged objectives;
- Clarify the feasibility of acquiring these resources.

⇒ *Feedback to the stakeholder (actor / beneficiary) analysis (2)*

⇒ *Feedback to objectives formulation (3)*

5. ANALYSIS OF EXTERNAL INFLUENCING FACTORS

- Explore external factors (in addition to supportive stakeholders) that may facilitate realisation of the programme or project (opportunities);

- Explore external factors (in addition to counter-working stake-holders) that may currently hinder the realisation of the programme or project (constraints);

- Explore external factors (in addition to counter-working stake-holders) that may pose problems in the future for the continuation of the programme or project, for maintenance of facilities created, or for the upkeep or augmentation of benefits generated (threats);

- Examine whether, to what extent and how the programme or project organisation(s) may exploit identified opportunities and counteract identified constraints and threats.

⇒ *Feedback to the problem analysis (1)*

⇒ *Feedback to the stakeholder (beneficiary / actor) analysis (2)*

⇒ *Feedback to objectives formulation (3)*

⇒ *Feedback to the resources assessment (4)*

6.   ASSESSMENT OF ORGANISATIONAL ABILITY

- Undertake an internal stakeholder analysis; i.e., examine the capabilities, interests and views of units and individuals in the responsible organisation(s);

- Clarify, in general terms,.necessary or desirable rules, structures, work systems and incentives of the responsible organisation(s) for undertaking the intended work;

- Indicate necessary or desirable measures (such as formal training, workshops and on-the-job training) for creating the needed or desirable organisational capabilities and for harmonising the interests and views of units and individuals in the organisation;

- Assess the feasibility of implementing such measures.

⇒ *Feedback to the stakeholder analysis (2)*

⇒ *Feedback to objectives formulation (3)*

⇒ *Feedback to the resources assessment (4)*

The main analytical categories in the table correspond directly or almost so with those in Figure 3.1 (in Section 1). There is a slight difference in terminology by the concept of 'stakeholder', introduced in Table 3.1 but not shown in Figure 3.1. In the context of that figure, stakeholders connect to 'problems' (primarily in the sense of people affected by them), to 'opportunities', 'constraints' and 'threats' (to the extent these refer to people or organisations), and even to 'organisation' (in the sense of units and individuals within the responsible organisation[s] who are involved). For further reflections about stakeholder analysis, see a couple of pages ahead.

The following are some important <u>additional issues</u> to those presented in the table:

Before starting any planning exercise, one needs to know *who are to be involved* in it, at least initially. This may mean to clarify:

- who is to be in overall charge of the planning (the organisation and the person within this);
- how broad the participation is to be within the overall responsible organisation;
- which other organisations, if any, are to be involved;
- which other groups and individuals, if any, are to be involved.

Together, the above concerns correspond to our just presented planning dimensions 'from above – from below' and 'excluding – participatory'.

If one finds, in the course of the planning exercise, that other actors should be involved than those who had been included from the beginning, one may consider bringing them in subsequently.

Moreover, it may be desirable or even necessary to undertake an *initial scanning* of the whole planning field, i.e., to conduct a general, relatively quick assessment of all the main aspects that one will have to address in the subsequent planning exercise. The purpose of this is to be confident that one continues to plan with a reasonable degree of certainty.

For instance, it may be futile to embark on any comprehensive problem, stakeholder and objectives analysis if there turns out to be no possibility of financing any measures or if money may be found only for measures for which no comprehensive strategic planning is needed.

In identifying the *core problem,* mentioned in point 1 in the table, one should go by the general principle that this problem should be at a high level in the means-ends chain that is conceptualised and presented (see also Section 6 of this chapter).

Commonly, the core problem may be referred to as the 'development problem', being at level with the 'development objective' of a corresponding programme or project.

However, programmes and, particularly, projects with less normative perspectives may not express an explicit concern with the living condition of people (which is implied in the notions of 'development problem' and 'development objective'), or they may emphasise relatively immediate achievements on the part of intended beneficiaries – such as increased knowledge or income – on which increased well-being may depend. In such cases, it will be appropriate to identify a core problem at a lower level, corresponding to an 'immediate objective' or even an 'output' of the development thrust.[10]

Readers who are experienced in strategy formulation will probably agree that problem analysis may be a complex endeavour indeed, in which the specification of one core problem may be very difficult – at least if people with different perspectives and interests are to arrive at a consensus about it. In particular, this may be the case for highly normative and comprehensive programmes. In such instances, it may be better to do away with the concept of 'core problem' altogether and emphasise the construction of a cause-effect network that makes sense to everybody. One should, of course, be able to identify an overall problem at the top of this network; this may, however, be too general and multifaceted to be meaningfully considered as the core problem.

---

[10] See Sections 6 and 7 for further elaboration of this argument.

Over the last few years, *stakeholder analysis* (see points 2 and 6 in the table) has come to be a much emphasised part of strategic planning. In relation to a development programme or project, we can define it generally as *an approach for gaining understanding by identifying the beneficiaries, key actors and other parties with interest in the programme or project, and assessing their respective stakes in that scheme* (see also Grimble and Chan [1995]).

A stakeholder analysis may well be seen as the most central element in the strategic planning of most development programmes and projects, as it links directly to and integrates most other components of the planning process. As clarified in Chapter One, development work focuses on groups of people, as beneficiaries, and frequently their institutions (being, then, the primary stakeholders), and problem analysis and objectives formulation make sense only in that perspective. The fact that the main attention in many projects is on more technical matters does not challenge this. Moreover, the various types of work under development programmes and projects are the responsibility of organisations and people in them, and resources are acquired from bodies with interest in the endeavour as well.[11]

We have earlier conceptualised various perspectives and courses of action in planning as 'planning modes' and we have linked the various mode-sets (dimensions) to our 'ground model' of strategy formulation, visualised in Figure 3.1.

However, the planning dimensions reflecting organisational 'rules' are less explicitly shown in both that framework and Table 3.1 than the other dimensions of planning. Most significantly, this is the case for the dimension of *blueprint - process*. Still, as emphasised in our presentation of that dimension in Section 2, clarification is essential about the degrees of flexibility in planning and whether

[11] The concept of stakeholder analysis has primarily been developed in relation to business management. A seminal contribution was that by Carroll (1989). The above mentioned article by Grimble and Chan (1995) contains an insightful discussion of the application of stakeholder analysis in development work, with direct reference to natural resource management.

one or more rounds of strategic planning will be undertaken. To a large extent, this should be clarified before any strategic planning starts, but the need for any additional strategic planning at later stages of a programme may be further clarified subsequently, through experiences gained during an initial planning process.

As mentioned earlier in this section, the *complexity* and *duration* of the planning exercise, including the importance and consequences of feedback information, will vary vastly between various programmes and projects.

It must be stressed that for many small and relatively simple thrusts, strategic planning need not be any long-lasting or comprehensive endeavour. The exercise must also be tailored to fit the abilities of people who are involved.

Usually, strategic planning of normative, comprehensive and integrated programmes is more demanding, will take a longer time, and will require more of a process approach than the planning of other programmes and projects, particularly if many and diverse participants are involved in the planning as well.

4. RELATED NOTIONS OF PLANNING

FRIEND AND JESSOP ON 'STRATEGIC CHOICE'

Decisions taken among possible options in planning have commonly been referred to as strategic choices.

For development organisations, choices of strategy usually mean to take decisions about courses of action in a complex, changing and, consequently, uncertain environment.

Three decades ago, J.K. Friend and W.N. Jessop (1969) made a comprehensive analysis of strategic choices in the public sector, which has achieved wide recognition among strategy orientated planners.

The focus in Friend and Jessop's analysis is on the various *uncertainties* which the public planner has to cope with. The authors specify three main kinds of such planning-related uncertainty:

- uncertainty about the planning environment – regarding its characteristics at the time of planning, future changes in it, and responses from it to interventions;
- uncertainty about future intentions of related actors – for instance, intentions by other government agencies;
- uncertainty about value judgements – because values, as held and expressed by different people in the society, cannot be measured and objectively compared with each other.

The planner's main challenge is, according to Friend and Jessop, to cope with these uncertainties as constructively as possible, in order to provide the final decision-takers with as comprehensive and clear an analysis as feasible, constituting the best possible foundation for the decisions to be arrived at.

For doing so, the planner must, as a first step, thoroughly explore the uncertainties relating to alternative courses of action. This must be done through an interactive process, for which qualitative methods of enquiry are needed. Next, the uncertainties must be clearly exposed; i.e., they must be made as visible and presented in as well sorted form as possible for the decision-takers.

The decision-takers should then express *immediate preferences* and identify *short-term courses of action* that are judged to be relatively safe. This is important both to ensure, as far as possible, that resources are used wisely and to maintain the public agency's accountability to its constituency (the people whom it is intended to serve).

Simultaneously, it will usually be important to *keep open several options* for action in the longer term, in order to exploit unforeseeable future opportunities as well as possible and to cope with future threats in the most effective manner.

Moreover, it is essential to *co-ordinate* choices of related agencies and for related agencies to work effectively together. In the same vein, any agency should be able to adjust its priorities and its mode of work in response to decisions and actions by other agencies.

Thus, good strategic choices will normally have to be made incrementally. Similar perspectives have subsequently come to be widely referred to as incremental planning or process planning (see also Section 2).[12]

FROM LONG-RANGE PLANNING TO CONTINUOUS STRATEGIC MANAGEMENT

One may distinguish between forms of strategic analysis by the length of the time horizon applied and, closely related, the specificity of and the degree of connectedness between the topics and issues addressed. The notions and perspectives involved may be better clarified through an examination of the following set of terms, found in literature on planning and management:

- Long-range planning
- Issue-focused planning
- Strategic management
- Environmental scanning.

These categories constitute an uneven continuum in terms of time horizons applied, from the relatively long-term to the relatively short-term, and embed related differences of specificity and interconnectedness of the variables dealt with.

Addressing the first three of these categories, Bryson and Einsweiler (1988) consider only the first two to be planning pursuits and only the second of them to be 'strategic planning'. Among the two categories, the first (long-range planning) focuses primarily on the 'specification of goals and objectives and their translation into current budgets and work programs', while the second (issue-focused planning) 'typically relies more on the identification and resolution of *issues*' (1988: 4).

This distinction is fruitful, in that it reflects a common difference in the extent to which interests of different groups (stakeholders)

---

[12]   The same ideas have been further developed by one of the authors with another co-author (Friend and Hickling [1997]).

and related conflicts are addressed in planning. Usually, long-range planning is done without much stakeholder analysis and assumes broad consensus about objectives. This may even be justified, by the general nature of the objectives which are formulated. Issue-focused planning, by its more selective, probing and action-orientated nature, is 'more suitable for politicized circumstances, since identifying and resolving issues do not presume an all-encompassing consensus on organizational purposes and actions' (Bryson and Einsweiler [1988: 4]). Thus, exploring interests and trying to resolve interest conflicts may be a major thrust of issue-focused planning.

Examples of long-range planning may be the formulation of long-term general plans (also referred to as 'perspective plans') for development of an economic or social sector, a region or a town. For instance, general town development plans may contain guidelines for physical expansion of the town, development of housing and infrastructure, and location of economic enterprises of various kinds. And these will be based on numerous assumptions, which in this case may be about population growth, composition of in-migrants, usage period of infrastructure, etc.

Sticking to the example of town development, issue-focused planning may be undertaken of many aspects, normally involving expression of and mediation between conflicting interests. One example may be efforts at integrating some ethnic group better into the social and political life of the town; another example may be efforts to re-classify zones within the town by their main function (such as residential and industrial), directly relating to present and future interests of several groups.

Unlike Bryson and Einsweiler, I do not see good reasons for considering only issue-focused planning as 'strategic'. Both long-range and issue-focused planning fit within the framework of strategic planning presented earlier in this chapter, while tending to emphasise different components of that framework.

The third category listed above, 'strategic management', is a much used while highly diverse and commonly also elusive concept. Having been primarily applied in the business world, it may be of less direct concern to most readers of this book. Occasionally, however, it is also used in the public sphere. Here, it tends to carry the notion of responding to demands in complex external environments, in contrast to a proactive plan formulation and decision-making process – whether of long-range or more issue-focused nature (see, for instance, Crow and Bozeman [1988]). Consequently, in strategic management, one tends to apply shorter time horizons' and to emphasise more specific issues in a less coherent manner than in either of the two previously mentioned types.

A related question, not discussed further, is how much of this may be referred to as 'planning', as this concept does imply an amount of pre-meditated action for initiation or regulation of societal processes and outcomes of these.

By 'environmental scanning' is usually meant a broad, relatively continuous and, commonly, focus-changing assessment of external factors of importance for an organisation or larger or smaller parts of the work that it undertakes, with the aim of responding as effectively as possible to external changes.

I perceive this as belonging more to the sphere of monitoring than to that of planning, and it is briefly addressed in that context in Chapter Six.

It should, though, be mentioned that 'environmental scanning' is sometimes used to denote the earliest steps of a strategic planning exercise, synonymously with 'initial scanning of the whole planning field', being a formulation I used in Section 3.

STRATEGIC VERSUS REGIONAL PLANNING

Most strategic planning is broad-focusing, which most planning for development of specified geographical areas also purports to be. The spatial planning units (areas) are commonly so-called functional regions, which may range from a basically rural area with a hierarchy of small centres to a major town with its hinterland.

Planning with focus on functional regions is commonly referred to as regional planning. It needs to be distinguished from local community planning, which may cover one local community, a cluster of a few adjoining communities, or several individual communities (often with similar features) over a larger area.

A further similarity between strategic and regional planning (besides the common feature of a broad focus) is that they both analyse relatively general aspects more than specific issues, the latter of which may be dealt with subsequently through more detailed sectoral or project planning (see shortly).

One may, therefore, be inclined to conceive of regional development planning as a specific application of strategic development planning.

There is, however, little empirical basis for linking the two in this way.

As stated by Dale (1999), regional development planning and the programmes which such planning commonly initiates have tended to be confined to physical and social infrastructure, standardised support facilities to individuals and groups and, sometimes, land use zoning, along with connected tasks such as compilation and processing of statistical data and statistical population projections.

This emphasis is, as also noted by Bryson and Einsweiler (1988), largely explained by the institutional context of the planning agencies, such as the legislation governing the planning, programme guidelines, and the location of planning agencies within government. Another explanatory factor is, no doubt, a heavy emphasis in much regional planning education on physical features and spatial planning techniques, which also tend to be linked to functional, blueprint and from-above perspectives.

In the present context, the main consequence of these points of emphasis is that broad problem, environment and stakeholder analysis, being usually crucial features of strategic planning, are commonly hardly undertaken or not pursued with much purpose and vigour in regional planning. Moreover, regional development plans tend to be comprehensive only in the sense of adding up relatively separate sectoral plans, each of which tends to be of basically functional (as juxtaposed to normative) nature.

Largely for such reasons, Dale (1999) argues that conventional regional development planning has tended to be a little effective mechanism for directing changes in the regions to which it is applied. This contrasts the lofty ambitions that are frequently expressed for regional planning thrusts, in terms of steering courses of development, according to some 'rational' principles on the part of the planners and the agencies which they represent.

INSTITUTION-CENTRED VERSUS OBJECT-CENTRED PERSPECTIVE

Faludi (1973a and 1973b) distinguishes between what he calls *procedural* and *object-centred* planning. Alternative terms for the latter, used by Faludi and others, are 'subject-matter' and 'substantive'.

The perspective on planning that has been presented in this chapter would, by this terminology, be primarily procedural: it focuses on the act of planning, i.e., broadly speaking, on how to identify and address people-related problems in the society, rather than on techniques of planning specific facilities or amenities (for instance, a road or a training scheme).

I prefer, though, to substitute the word 'procedural' with some alternative term, which better reflects the breadth of issues involved and in addition does not contain the notion of formalism that lies in 'procedural'. *Institution-centred* is, in my view, a term that satisfies these criteria.

STRATEGIC VERSUS OPERATIONAL AND ADJUSTIVE PLANNING

Strategic planning needs to be supplemented with planning of more detailed nature. And detailed plans sometimes have to be modified. Common terms for such additional planning are 'operational' and 'adjustive' planning respectively.

Operational planning means further specification of a range of features and processes than is done in the preceding strategic planning. A good operational plan should be a firm, detailed and clear guide for implementation. Usually, in operational planning, main emphasis is needed on the intended outputs as well as on aspects of organisation and resource use.

The following is a somewhat more detailed, while not exhaustive, list of aspects that commonly need to be elaborated through subsequent operational planning:

- Geographical area/localities and beneficiaries;
- Outputs, when relevant with detailed design;
- Implementation: tasks, actors and their roles, detailed procedures, time schedule;
- Technology to be applied in implementation;
- Finances: detailed budget, payment system, expenditure recording system;
- Monitoring: tasks, actors and their roles, procedures, progress recording and reporting system;
- Evaluation arrangements;
- Reward system, personnel training, and other personnel related aspects;
- Benefit-cost relation;
- Sustainability of organisation, work processes, facilities and/or benefits.

Adjustive planning means modifications of existing plans, normally in the course of implementation, within an intended unchangeable framework of aims and modes of operation that have normally been established in those plans. Thus, the scope of adjustive planning to modify plans is usually strictly limited but may vary substantially.

5. PROJECTS AND PROGRAMMES

In previous pages, I have already used the words 'project' and 'programme' several times. This is because they tend to be the most frequently used terms for denoting planned and organised work for societal development. For this reason and because the words are neither synonymous nor interchangeable, we need to have their meanings better clarified.

PROJECTS

The term 'project' is commonly used in a rather loose sense, denoting some piece of work which is to be done under some constraints of time and resources. In relation to organised endeavours, including development work, the usage is normally more precise. In such contexts, definitions of 'project' abound.[13]

In general accord with other definitions, I will broadly define a development project as *a planned intervention for achieving one or more objectives, encompassing a set of interrelated activities which are undertaken during a delimited period of time, using specified human, financial and physical resources.*

Thus, development projects, like other endeavours which use resources that must be accounted for, should be well specified before starting to implement any components, leaving as little uncertainty as possible about achievements and their costs. By implication, for a development intervention to be termed a project, it should be formulated in a *blueprint* mode, through *operational* planning.

PROGRAMMES

A 'programme' is a less clearly bounded entity. We can most easily define it in relation to a project, as *a less specified and commonly more comprehensive, long-term and/or diverse intervention.*

In the perspective of our basic categories of development planning, a programme may have been formulated through *strategic* planning only, and it may in principle be located at any point on a *blueprint – process* continuum.

Programmes and projects are often related in that development work under a programme is further operationalised in one or more additional plan documents, which may be referred to as project documents. Sometimes, such specifications are instead made within

---

[13]   Wickramanayake (1993) presents some such definitions.

the programme document itself. In yet other cases, specifications may be left to local organisations or user groups, possibly outside the responsible programme organisation, which may not document all or even any of the specifications. Examples may be programmes for supplying credit, other production inputs or housing materials to local community groups.

Broadly speaking, we may distinguish between the following two types of development programmes, by their scope:

One-sector programmes

These are programmes containing activities within the same sector. 'Sector' is normally defined by the criterion of administrative responsibility, such as education, fisheries or agricultural extension. Programmes thus delimited are commonly simply referred to as sector programmes.

One-sector programmes may be:

- *standardised*, i.e., having pre-specified activities and outputs (which means that they are planned in a *blueprint* mode);
- more *flexible*; i.e., their contents or processes (as usually further specified in subsequent operational planning) may be allowed to vary – for instance, between localities – or allowed to change (which means that they are planned in more of a *process* mode).

Multi-sector programmes

These are programmes containing activities in several sectors (which means that they are more *comprehensive,* sector-wise).

Multi-sector programmes may also be *standardised* or more or less *flexible*. In addition, they may be, to different extents:

- *disjointed*, containing activities which are not or not substantially related to each other;
- more *integrated*, containing activities which are functionally related to each other and which may in addition focus on the same people.

Most multi-sector programmes cover one contiguous geographical area or selected localities within one delimited area.

There may also be hierarchies of programmes. For instance, a development programme that covers one district may contain several divisional programmes, each of which may contain local community programmes. Within this hierarchy, projects may be planned and implemented at any level.

Please note that the term 'programme' is also frequently used with a different meaning, in the phrase 'work programme'. A work programme spells out implementation details of a project or parts of it. Linked to this is 'programming', meaning detailed specification and sequencing of activities.

6. MEANS-ENDS RELATIONS

The concerns of a development programme or project can be specified through chains of means and ends.

In compliance with its *strategy*, the development organisation should specify the envisaged *outputs* of the work that it intends to do along with the *inputs* and *tasks of implementation* for creating the outputs. Since the outputs should serve some development purpose, this purpose should be clarified and specified as well. The purpose is commonly expressed as *immediate objectives* and *development objective*. By common development terminology, these correspond to *intended effects* and *intended impacts* respectively. 'Immediate objectives' and 'effects' denote fairly direct benefits of the outputs, whereas 'development objective' and 'impacts' signify more indirect benefits, commonly materialising over a longer period.

Only one development objective should be formulated. Some argue for only one immediate objective also. However, for broad-based schemes, this may mean that the latter would have to be formulated in highly general terms as well. I find this recommendation unnecessarily constraining, and I propose that planners should feel free to formulate more than one immediate objective.[14]

---

[14] With reference to our discussion of 'core problem' in Section 3, formulating more than one immediate objective should definitely be advantageous

Since the intention of any development work is to address some problem relating to some people, the development objective must always and the immediate objectives should usually directly connect achievements with people; i.e., express the benefits that are intended to accrue to the intended beneficiaries (see Section 7 for examples).

Linking the above to our concepts of 'normative' and 'functional' planning, the development objective and, therewith, the impacts are of more explicit concern to a development organisation the more normative its endeavour is.

In plans for development projects that are located towards the functional end on the normative – functional continuum, one *assumes* that the intervention is significant for the well-being of people, rather than analyses the links between the project outputs and such benefits. Consequently, for such projects, it may be argued that specification of a development objective may often not serve much purpose and may, therefore, not be appropriate.[15]

On the other hand, such an objective is, by direct implication, essential for programmes of highly normative nature.

For many normative programmes and projects, one may also add the very general notion of *self-sustained development*. With this is meant that the benefits of a programme or project are not only expected to be maintained after the termination of the intervention, but that those benefits (for instance, increased income) are envisaged to be further augmented in a self-sustained process, for the original target group or for other people.

---

if these objectives connect to a development objective that corresponds to an agreed core problem. In such cases, formulating more than one immediate objective would be the corollary of formulating more than one cause of that problem.

[15] Still, since funding agencies of development programmes and projects need to justify their support through envisaged benefits for specified people, these agencies tend to routinely require a development objective to be formulated even for projects for which impacts and even effects may not have been substantially analysed.

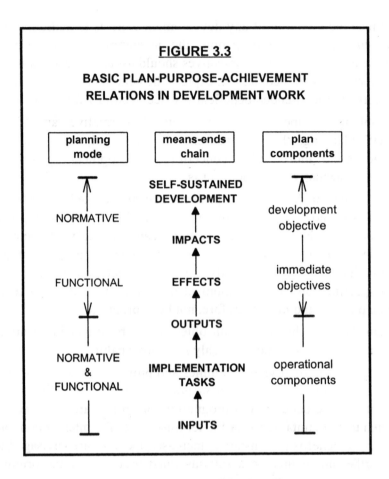

FIGURE 3.3

BASIC PLAN-PURPOSE-ACHIEVEMENT
RELATIONS IN DEVELOPMENT WORK

planning mode	means-ends chain	plan components
	SELF-SUSTAINED DEVELOPMENT	development objective
NORMATIVE	IMPACTS	
FUNCTIONAL	EFFECTS	immediate objectives
	OUTPUTS	
NORMATIVE & FUNCTIONAL	IMPLEMENTATION TASKS	operational components
	INPUTS	

A general means-ends chain of development programmes and projects is visualised in Figure 3.3. For the sake of perspective, this is related to our planning dimension of normative – functional and to major plan components.

The main pieces of information contained in the figure and reflections relating to it are:

Since any development work aims at producing some output using some resources, *inputs, tasks of implementation* and *outputs* will be specified in any operational plan, irrespective of how functional or normative the perspective is.

Immediate intended results for people (*effects*) would also be expected to be assessed in any planning exercise, at least cursorily, and corresponding immediate objectives would be expected to be formulated. Still, we have stated, in some instances the organisation in charge may not make much effort to analyse links between outputs and effects and may not try to verify whether or to what extent such effects materialise. In such cases, the concern of the planning agency (which may or may not be in charge of implementation as well) in reality ends at the output level (implying planning in a highly functional mode), making even immediate objectives less significant.

Conversely, the more the planning agency analyses intended changes in people's well-being (*impacts*) and makes efforts to verify to what extent these materialise (i.e., the more normative the planning is), the more essential is the inclusion of clearly formulated objectives in the plan document or documents.

Such means-ends chains are frequently presented in what is commonly called a *logical framework* or – for projects – a *project matrix*. The two main purposes are usually to help structure the analysis and to promote an understanding among relatively peripheral stakeholders or outsiders about the purpose and measures of the programme or project.

In addition to means-ends relations, specified by the categories that we have used above, the logical framework incorporates (a) external (environmental) conditions for fulfilling the objectives and (b) indicators of achievements.

External factors are variables over which the programme or project management has no or, at most, very limited influence, which may affect 'conversions' from one level to the next in the means-ends chain (for instance, to what extent and how outputs get converted into effects). Examples may be the influence of any weather changes on the survival and growth of tree seedlings, and the influence of a range of cultural factors (not being addressed in the respective programme or project) on the adoption of new disease preventing practices that are promoted.

Indicators are brief, concise expressions, serving as simplified approximations of effects, impacts and/or sustainability. We resort to indicators when the reality – in this context primarily operational performance, effects or impacts – is too comprehensive or complex to be studied in its entirety. A couple of examples may be: attendance in meetings as an approximation of participation in decision-making, and arm circumference as an approximation of the nutritional status of children.[16]

For development programmes or projects, specification of means-ends chains tends to result in a *hierarchical* structure of means and ends. In other words, the realisation of one factor at any level commonly depends on the realisation of more than one factor (often many more) at the next lower level. For instance, several tasks may be required to produce one output. This is further illustrated in the second of the two examples which will be presented in the next section.

Generally speaking, the development organisation will have a high *degree of control* at the lowest levels (i.e., over the inputs, implementation tasks and outputs) and decreasing control as we move further up in the chain or hierarchy. In other words, external factors tend to exert stronger influence the higher up in the hierarchy we come. This issue, as well, is further illustrated in the second example of the next following section.

However, the degree of organisational control or influence at different levels depends heavily on a number of variables, such as: the field of intervention, how normative the perspective is, other strategic choices made, the character of the organisation (for instance, whether public benefit or mutual benefit), the capacity and competence of the organisation, and numerous aspects in the organisation's environment.

---

[16] The logical framework, including external factors and indicators, is not elaborated more here. A simple description and discussion of basic features is provided in Dale (1998). Versions of the logical framework are also used by virtually all major aid agencies.

7. TWO EXAMPLES

In this section, I will further clarify main issues of strategy formulation for development through two examples. In both cases, the main focus is on means-ends relations, with linked reflections about other connected aspects of strategy.

The first example is presented in Box 3.1.

Besides illustrating aspects of strategy which have been explored in the present chapter, this case also connects to Chapter Two, in that it involves three kinds of *organisations* – a local community organisation, a non-governmental organisation and a government department – which intend to co-operate in a development programme. It further links the set of means-ends categories that we addressed in the preceding section with the concepts of *vision* and *mission*, also defined in Chapter Two and additionally referred to in Section 1 of the present chapter.

Moreover, the development thrust that is presented here invites reflections about the essential distinction between *programmes* and *projects* and the often widely different perspectives one may need to apply in the planning of these two main categories of development work.

Seen in its entirety, the venture described in the box is, unquestionably, a programme. It is even expected to last over any foreseeable future, while having no specified resource requirements beyond an establishment phase. Two of the organisations (the LCO and the GD) are intended to maintain responsibility over such an unspecified future. These continuing activities, intended to be undertaken beyond the establishment phase, are italicised in the box.

Thus, as seen at the time of planning, only the NGO is intended to have a time-bound involvement. The duration of that involvement may be specified in advance, or the time of termination may be decided on at some later point in time. The period of engagement in one community will most probably be pre-specified. In this case, it may be two years, encompassing establishment activities and the subsequent intended monitoring of the pre-school activities for one

---

BOX 3.1

A COMMUNITY-BASED PRE-SCHOOL PROGRAMME

The scenario is a programme that is being planned for establishment and running of pre-schools (preparatory education facilities for primary school) in local communities in a district of a country. The programme is intended to be a collaborative effort between one local community organisation (LCO) in each of the programme communities, a non-governmental organisation (NGO), and a government department (GD).

During the stage of strategic planning, it has been decided that, in each community, each of the co-operating organisations will contribute to the programme as follows:

LCO	NGO	GD
Organise a one-week motivation campaign in the community	Supply material for the motivation campaign	
	Conduct the motivation campaign	
Establish pre-school committee of the LCO	Conduct training course for the pre-school committee	
Recruit persons to be pre-school teachers	Train two persons as pre-school teachers	*Pay the salary of two pre-school teachers*
Erect a pre-school building with related facilities	Advise on construction and approve the building	
	Provide teaching material	
	Monitor school operation for one year	
Maintain the pre-school building	Contribute to maintenance fund	
Operate the pre-school		

For meaningful co-operation, the participating organisations must have a common set of objectives. This set may be linked to a vision and a mission. In this case, these have been stated as follows:

Vision
A society in which children of all social groups are mentally well prepared for formal education.

Mission
Preparing as many children as possible for formal education, with particular emphasis on children from the poorest households.

Development objective
The majority of children in the programme communities, also from the poorest households, being substantially better prepared, intellectually and emotionally, for primary education.

Immediate objectives
1. At least 80% of the children of 3–5 years in each programme community attend the pre-school regularly;
2. At least one fourth of the attending children in each community come from the poorest one fourth of the households;
3. The attending children are receiving the intended care and impulses for mental development.

In fulfilment of this set of objectives, each organisation will have separate but complementary sets of inputs, tasks and outputs. Reflecting its intended contribution, the planned outputs of the NGO's activities in each community have been stated as follows – all according to specified times and schedules for each activity:

a. The motivation campaign has been completed, using the standard set of campaign material;
b. The designed training course for the committee has been conducted;
c. Two persons from the community have been given the full preschool teachers' training course;
d. Completion of a pre-school building and related facilities of satisfactory standard [as specified separately] have been ascertained;
e. The package of teaching material has been provided;
f. The quality of teaching during the first year has been ascertained;
g. The agreed contribution to the maintenance fund has been made to the pre-schools meeting the criteria [specified separately].

year. One may then also assume that the contribution to the maintenance fund will be done after verification of successful operation of the school during this one-year monitoring period.

On the other hand, while time-limited, the period of the NGO's involvement in the programme as a whole may or may not be predetermined. This strategic choice may decide whether the NGO's contribution may be most appropriately called a programme or a project of the NGO (constituting one part of the entire programme).

If the NGO's involvement is open-ended, this is obviously a programme (or, in the context of the entire thrust, a sub-programme). If a time-frame is specified at the inception, it may be referred to as either a programme or a project, largely depending on whether or not the organisation will specify all its intended activities over the entire period and prepare cost estimates for all of them in advance (connecting to our notions of blueprint and process planning respectively). If it does so, it will also have to limit in advance the number of pre-schools it will support, for instance, a pre-determined number per year.

A note may be warranted on *outputs*. As stated in the figure, each participating organisation will have its own set of outputs, resulting from activities undertaken by each of them individually. Additionally, one may conceptualise a common output above these individual sets. An appropriately formulated common output from those created by the organisations individually would be 'the pre-school is operational'.

A further clarification of such multiple levels within one category is made in our next case.

Also, note the inter-relationship (the two-way cause-effect link in the figure) between 'mission' and 'objectives'. The set of objectives of the present programme is shown to be guided by a more general mission of the participating organisations. Conversely, as indicated by the second arrow, the mission may be influenced by work that the organisations are involved in – although it would not be expected to change frequently from experiences gained from such work.

As discussed earlier, an even more general notion of 'mission' is the overall purpose of the organisation's existence and, therewith, of anything that it does or intends to do. Among the present set of organisations, we would expect the NGO, at least, to have a formulated general (organisation-wide) mission.

Sustainability is a matter of major concern in such a programme. There is bound to be substantial uncertainty attached to the running of the pre-schools by the LCOs, in some communities probably more so than in others, and the more the further into the future one looks. This may also be the case for long-term financial support by the GD.

The programme authorities should carefully consider future threats to sustainability and should, whenever feasible, devise measures to counteract them. Such measures may be implemented during the establishment phase or even after it. In this case, an example of the former is the contribution to a maintenance fund (stated in the box). An example of the latter may be some contingency arrangement by the NGO, in terms of a preparedness plan to help solve problems that may emerge later, which may be activated at any time.

The second example, shown in Figure 3.4, presents means-ends chains of a project or programme (depending on perspective and scope) for addressing problems of paddy cultivating farmers under an irrigation scheme that is silted up through erosion from its water catchment, for which depletion of the forest cover is viewed to be a cause. I will use this example to illustrate three main issues relating to means-ends thinking.

The first issue is the relation between *core intended achievement* and *activity scope*. The 'core intended achievement' may be viewed as equivalent to the 'core problem' in a corresponding problem analysis. In a development context, the level of the 'core intended achievement' also reflects the location of the programme or project on a normative-functional continuum.

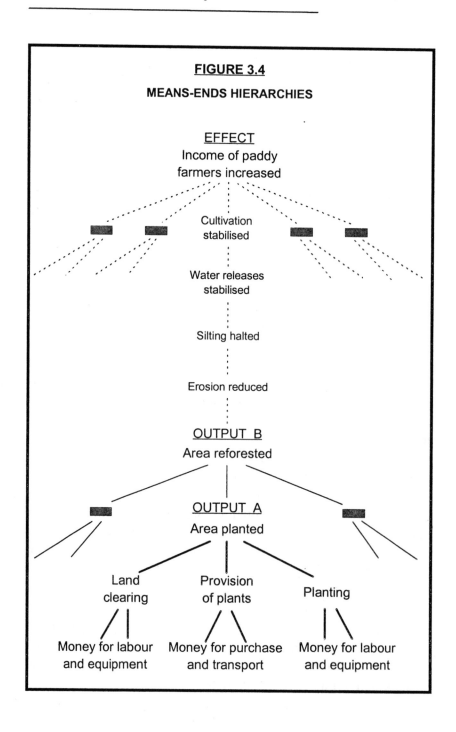

FIGURE 3.4

MEANS-ENDS HIERARCHIES

EFFECT
Income of paddy
farmers increased

Cultivation
stabilised

Water releases
stabilised

Silting halted

Erosion reduced

OUTPUT B
Area reforested

OUTPUT A
Area planted

Land
clearing

Provision
of plants

Planting

Money for labour
and equipment

Money for purchase
and transport

Money for labour
and equipment

In order to clarify this crucial issue, let us have a look at different scenarios.

First, we assume that the concern of the responsible organisation is to have the water catchment planted with new seedlings – which would, in due course, be expected to reforest the area. 'Area planted' is, clearly, a result at the *output* level, and one which the development agency should be able to guarantee. Successful realisation of this endeavour would, then, depend on a narrow set of inputs and implementation tasks, illustrated in the figure by the set of variables connected by thick lines.

This first scenario is, clearly, that of a project, and one that is planned in a strongly functional mode.

Next, let us shift our focus to augmentation of the income of farmers who are cultivating under the irrigation system, being an achievement at the *effect* level (expressing benefits for specified people). While the programme or project may still include reforestation of the water catchment, in order to improve the cultivation through reduced silting of reservoirs and canals, it may also involve a number of other interventions (i.e., be more comprehensive), illustrated in the figure by the set of dotted lines. These may be other activities relating to paddy cultivation (for instance, credit supply and cultivation advice) and even more different activities, inside or outside the field of agriculture. We have, to keep the figure simple, extended the means-ends relations of such additional components a couple of levels downward only; this should, however, be sufficient for clarifying the argument.

We have here a much more normative development thrust. It may be referred to as a programme or as a project, depending on the extent to which inputs, activities and outputs are pre-specified.

This same issue is also illustrated, to a more limited extent, by shifting our attention to the much shorter leap upward from 'area planted' to 'area reforested'. In doing so, additional measures may be required to safeguard against or reduce external threats to growth of the trees, examples of which may be fires, grazing, encroachment for cultivation, and diseases. Such safeguards may be implemented at the time of planting (for instance, preparing fire protection lines through clearing of vegetation) or over a subsequent period (for instance, through a watcher service and linked contingency plans for additional action if and when needed).

It is this relation between project *internal* and *external* factors that I primarily want to illustrate through this last-mentioned shift. Generally, as stated, external factors exert stronger influence the higher up in means-ends chains we move.

Still, in this case, 'reforested' is also an achievement at the output level only, albeit above 'planted': even 'reforested' does not embed any notion of benefits for people.

This, in turn, links to the third point which I want to make: that the *number of levels* in means-ends chains may be many more than the five that we have distinguished between and which are commonly incorporated in the logical framework (inputs, implementation tasks, outputs, immediate objectives and development objective). This is further illustrated in the figure by the chain 'erosion reduced – silting halted – water releases stabilised – cultivation stabilised'. Whether one wants to consider such additional means/ ends as located within one of the logical framework categories or as located between them, may be a matter of individual preference.

Relating to our analysis of the concept of 'development' in Chapter One, we have so far addressed organisations involved in development work and how the organisations may conceptualise and specify their pursuits. The latter has been done under the broad concepts of 'strategy formulation' and 'strategic planning', which have been juxtaposed to related notions of planning and broken down into their elements, the relations between which have also been explored. More specifically, we have connected problems to be addressed and objectives of the organisations' work to environmental opportunities and constraints, resources at the organisations' disposal, and a range of organisation-specific variables. There is now a need to analyse further these components of organisation. This will be our concern in the following chapter.

Chapter Four

ORGANISATIONAL FEATURES AND WORK CATEGORIES

1. ORGANISATIONAL VARIABLES IN DEVELOPMENT PERSPECTIVE

In Figure 4.1 I have connected the main categories of planning, addressed in the previous chapter, to the general means-ends chain of development work, also presented in that chapter. I have further illustrated how achievements may be influenced by external factors, the more so the higher up in the means-ends chain we move (illustrated by increasing thickness of the influence arrows).

To these main categories I have then added features of organisations and additional categories of organised work, to be explored in this chapter.

Strategic planning is shown to be undertaken through an interlinked analysis of factors in the organisation's environment (problems to be addressed, opportunities, constraints and threats), objectives of the development work, resources and organisation, as spelt out in Chapter Three. This is followed by operational planning – largely emphasising output design, issues of organisation and resource use. Resources are, through operational planning, specified as inputs for the development work to be done. The inputs are, through implementation, converted into outputs. The outputs are, in

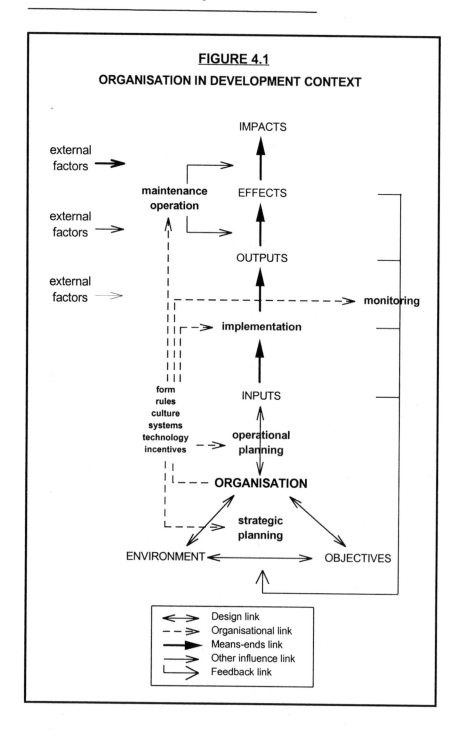

FIGURE 4.1

ORGANISATION IN DEVELOPMENT CONTEXT

IMPACTS

external factors

maintenance operation

EFFECTS

external factors

OUTPUTS

external factors

monitoring

implementation

form
rules
culture
systems
technology
incentives

INPUTS

operational planning

ORGANISATION

strategic planning

ENVIRONMENT

OBJECTIVES

← →	Design link
– – ⇒	Organisational link
➡	Means-ends link
→	Other influence link
⌐→	Feedback link

turn, expected to produce some changes in the society, referred to as effects and impacts.

The main work processes of planning, implementation, operation, maintenance and monitoring are visualised as organised endeavours, through their link with the 'organisation' category. These processes will be referred to as organisational 'functions' (see also later).

Information about the work undertaken and the immediate outcome of that work is generated and fed back into planning through the function of monitoring.[1]

'Organisation' carries two inter-related notions: *responsibility* and *ability*:

One or more organisations are responsible for planning and, subsequently, implementation and monitoring, as well as any operation and maintenance that may be done. To be able to perform these functions, the organisations structure themselves physically in specific ways, and they apply rules, systems of administration, technologies and personnel incentives. All these features are, to varying extents, interconnected with aspects of the organisations' culture.

These organisational variables influence, directly and strongly, the processes and the quality of work and, thereby, the achievements of any development endeavour.

---

[1] One usually distinguishes between two main mechanisms of providing such feedback: monitoring and evaluation.

Monitoring is normally done, at least mainly, by programme- or project-responsible organisations. It basically means frequent collection and analysis of information in the course of programme or project implementation, in order to ascertain whether the scheme is on the right course and implemented well, and to help the responsible persons take any corrective action. It usually emphasises processes of work and outputs, but may also encompass assessment of effects. We shall revert to this function later in this chapter and in Chapter Six.

'Evaluation' is a more comprehensive concept with greater analytical challenges, to which we shall devote a whole chapter (Chapter Six).

2. THE CONCEPT OF ORGANISATIONAL FORM

An organisation's 'form' denotes the number and types of sub-units of the organisation and relations of work between these units. It reflects the variety of functions and tasks of the organisation and predominant patterns of communication, responsibility and power.

Somewhat more specifically, we may define it as: *the set of roles[2] performed by individuals, commonly grouped into divisions, departments or similar units around functions, commodities, services, regions or markets, and the distribution of power across this role structure.*

Our concept of organisational 'form' broadly corresponds to some authors' conception of organisational 'structure'. In fact, the just stated definition is a slightly modified version of that by Galbraith and Kazanjian (1986) of the structure of organisations.

Simultaneously, 'structure' is frequently used with broader connotations, and it is often rather vaguely defined, even in organisational contexts.

I have, therefore, avoided the term 'structure' for expressing the relatively specific dimension of organisation which is presently addressed, therewith also reserving the term for broader and more flexible usage.

Figure 4.2 shows a highly general framework of the main parts of organisations and the way they are interconnected, as commonly presented in literature on organisations. This simple framework constitutes a good basis for analysing the form of various kinds of organisations, whether or not the respective bodies contain all or only some of the parts that are specified.

The vertical axis, connecting the operating core, the middle management and the top management (commonly also referred to as the

---

[2] The 'role' of a person or a group of persons denotes what that person or group is expected to do or actually does, in relation to what others (in the organisation, in this context) are expected to do or actually do.

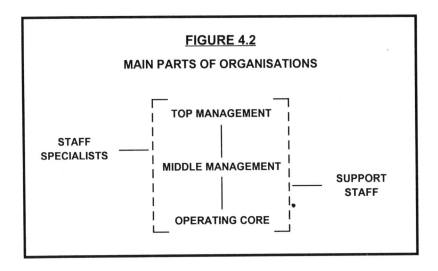

FIGURE 4.2

MAIN PARTS OF ORGANISATIONS

'strategic apex'), is frequently termed the organisation's *line*. The staff specialists (alternatively referred to by organisation analysts as 'advisers' or the 'techno-structure') and the support staff are together commonly termed the organisation's *staff*.

As will be substantiated shortly, this framework is directly applicable for typically bureaucratic organisations, while other organisational types may deviate from this ground-model to different extents. However, at least a couple of the categories specified in the figure can normally be identified in any type of organisations, except in organisations that I will, a couple of pages ahead, refer to as 'collectives'. The last-mentioned bodies may be considered to consist of only one of the entities shown, namely the operating core.

Very briefly, we can define each of these main parts of organisations as follows:

Organisational line

This is the vertical axis of the organisation, the units of which undertake work in direct fulfilment of the organisation's objectives. Many of the people here have, to various extents, authority to take decisions about strategy, processes of work or individual tasks.

Operating core

The operating core of the organisation directly produces the commodities or services that the organisation provides to its customers or other target groups.

Top management

This body is charged with the overall responsibility for the activities and achievements of the organisation, including decisions about its general strategy, the way it structures itself physically and divides up its work (i.e., its form), and operational and administrative procedures. It also executes general control of the organisation's performance. The latter is done through various measures that are commonly referred to as co-ordination mechanisms, including that of 'direct supervision'.[3]

Middle management

This links the operating core to the top management. It consists of persons who have decision-making authority in specific fields, i.e., for the work tasks of units which they head.[4]

Staff specialists

These persons are a support facility for the units in the organisation's line. They are analysts who may advise managers on a range of topics and issues, design administrative systems for the organisation, etc. A major concern of theirs is often to promote 'standardisation' of

---

[3]   Mechanisms of co-ordination are crucial for harmonising pieces of work in most organisations and for making sub-units and their individuals pull in the same direction. Such mechanisms will be addressed in Section 8 of this chapter.

[4]   Linked to the management structure of organisations (addressed here) is the process denoting noun 'management' (from the verb 'manage'). For an elaboration of the latter, see Section 6.

A similar dual usage applies for 'administration', which is commonly used interchangeably with 'management', denoting:

    (a) the parts of the organisation which administer;
    (b) the process of administering.

work processes or the outputs of these processes, being commonly also referred to as a mechanism of co-ordination.

Support staff

Persons of this category may provide a variety of non-advisory services, examples of which may be printing, payment of staff and accounting.

3. MAJOR FORMS OF DEVELOPMENT ORGANISATIONS

In terms of physical set-up and authority relations, organisations are structured in vastly different ways. Numerous forms may be identified, depending on the focus, scope and depth of the analysis.[5]

The typology presented over the next few pages is considered to encompass and distinguish reasonably well between main forms of organisations in the development field (while also having wider applicability, in full or partly).[6] Most development organisations are considered to unambiguously belong to one of the presented categories, and almost all such organisations are at least primarily characterised by features of one of these forms. In a few instances, though, placement of an organisation may not be obvious, as it may contain a mixture of major aspects of a couple of the forms.

---

[5] Consequently, analysts have suggested numerous formats for classification. Some apply a broad 'systems' perspective, embedding dimensions of strategy, form and other organisational features. Scott (1987) provides one such perspective, defining organisations by the major criteria of purpose, form, behaviour and influence as rational systems, natural systems and open systems respectively. Readers who want to explore aspects of organisational structure more in-depth, are particularly requested to delve into the inspiring writings of Henry Mintzberg, a couple of which are mentioned in the next footnote. A summary of Mintzberg's main ideas (along with those of many other organisation analysts) is found in Pugh and Hickson (1997).

[6] Inputs to the following presentation are provided by, in particular, Mintzberg (1983; 1989), Cusworth and Franks (1993) and AIT (1998). However, the typology is my own, building largely on experience from working in and with development organisations.

THE COLLECTIVE

This is a group of people who work together on relatively equal terms for a common purpose, and do so more than casually. That is, they collaborate over a substantial period of time, performing tasks that are regulated to larger or lesser extents. The regulatory mechanisms may, however, be entirely or largely informal.

Along with involvement on basically equal terms, the genuine collective is *characterised* by a fully interconnected pattern of communication, with no one performing the role of leader.

However, there is a slightly deviating form, having what we may refer to as a 'convenience manager' or 'group representative'. With this is meant that one person acts as the organisation's formal head for basically pragmatic reasons. One such reason may be to facilitate contacts and dealings with external bodies, another may be to administer common internal affairs more efficiently. Often, the role of representative rotates.

The criteria by which such a headed organisation is still considered to be a collective, are that most decisions are taken collectively and that the members do not divide up work, by its kind, among themselves to any large extent. This usually also implies that co-ordination of the group's affairs is mainly or largely done through mutual adjustment (see Section 8).

This form is *suitable* only for small organisations performing relatively simple and similar jobs.[7]

The main *examples* of collectives of a *non-headed* nature in the development field are various kinds of small local community groups, commonly established fairly spontaneously for some rather specific purpose, such as to protect the interests of the members in the face of an external threat, to jointly exploit a resource, or to augment the members' income. These collectives are usually independent, and many of them may not be very long-lasting. Often, the persons may be so loosely connected or their common activities

---

[7]   A 'job' is defined as a cluster of closely related tasks.

may be so sporadic that it may be a matter of judgement whether their group should be considered as an organisation at all.

The *headed* sub-form is also most often found in local communities. Many organisations with a formally instituted representative are formed under some government policy or development programme, and they are then commonly expected to relate to external bodies (such as other programme units, banks or government agencies) in their work. Others may be locally initiated groups, the members of which have for some reason found it advantageous to formalise a representation role, for purposes such as to facilitate expansion or to establish new relations outwards.

The main *advantages* of collectives are the uncomplicated process of establishment, the simplicity of internal dealings, and the democratic features of the organisation, which under certain conditions may also be empowering.[8]

THE ONE-LEADER BODY

This is an organisation having one person in direct charge of major decisions and functions. This person's position is, thus, fundamentally different from that of the convenience manager just mentioned. Appropriate designations for this position and the connected role are *leader* and *leadership*.

In the one-leader organisation, the operation and survival of the organisation depends largely or even mainly on this person at the top. The person's sphere of influence may range from ideological guidance to direct and detailed control of current operations. Commonly, the leader is also the initiator and main creator of the organisation, in which case we may refer to the person as a 'foundation leader'.

There are numerous *examples* of organisations with foundation leaders in the NGO sphere. Most of them are small. Some continue to be led by this all-important person for the lifetime of either the organisation or its leader – or both. Others, particularly those which

---

[8] For definition and discussion of 'empowerment', see Chapter Five.

grow substantially, change their form and system of management and may after some time become widely different organisations from what they were initially.

In this type of organisation, the ideological spirit of the leader is commonly essential not only for formation of the organisation (if the leader founded or was involved in founding it), but also for ensuring good work. Such ideological influence is often complemented with other leadership abilities and sometimes also specific technical competence on the part of the leader. Herein lies the basic *rationale* of this organisational form. An additional advantage is its simplicity, which may enhance organisational efficiency.

In some instances, however, re-orientation and organisational renewal, which may become advantageous or even necessary after some period of existence, may be stifled by the all-embracing influence of one person.

THE HIERARCHY

This is the most common form of bigger organisations, in the development sphere and elsewhere.

Typically hierarchical organisations have one person in overall charge at the top and an increasing number of units and individuals at successively lower levels. Each unit at any level has a manager, being responsible for that unit as well as linked units at lower levels (implying a supervisory role vis-à-vis the managers of those sub-units as well). The number of levels, the number of units at each level, and how even or 'neat' the hierarchical shape is may be influenced by numerous variables, among which the size of the organisation may be particularly important.

The hierarchical form is closely linked to the notion of *bureaucracy*. Besides the hierarchical arrangement of units (offices) and the corresponding differentiation of authority and responsibilities, just mentioned, the core features of typical bureaucracies are:

- specialisation of tasks and jobs and corresponding skills in performing those tasks and jobs;

- all the work performed according to clearly specified rules and procedures;
- recruitment of personnel according to professional criteria only;
- impersonal norms governing work relations between the people in the organisation.[9]

Of course, these features are not limited to hierarchically built organisations, and may be desirable with other organisational forms as well. They are, however, seen as essential for proper functioning of hierarchical bodies, and constitute together with the hierarchical form what we may call a bureaucratic configuration.

Big bureaucratic organisations will normally have a substantial number of staff employed, both specialists (advisers) and various kinds of support staff (see Figure 4.2), commonly working in clearly defined units that may themselves also be hierarchically structured.

The bureaucratic organisational configuration carries unquestionable *qualities,* essential to much development work. Prime among these are: equality of treatment according to set criteria, predictability and accountability (assuming, of course, that the bureaucratic principles are adhered to). With their clearly specified objectives, jobs, work tasks and work routines, bureaucracies are also particularly well suited to undertake pieces of work that are repetitive or similar, also on a large scale. Moreover, the bureaucratic principles help ensure security of employment and fair treatment of the personnel of the organisation.

Major *weaknesses* may be lack of innovative ability (due to the rigidity of structures and procedures), narrow technical perspectives (linked to detailed specification of tasks and high specialisation of skills), inefficient resource use (because of cumbersome procedures or because contributions by individuals may not be clearly exposed

---

[9] The concept of 'bureaucracy' was comprehensively developed by the German lawyer and sociologist Max Weber (1864–1920). It is particularly well elaborated in the following book, first published in 1924: *The Theory of Social and Economic Organization;* Free Press. (Reprints 1947 and 1961.)

in the maze of interactions), and difficult access to the organisation for outsiders (due to high formality of relations).

There are, however, great variations in the degrees of freedom that all or most of the personnel of hierarchical organisations have. Such differences may be broadly expressed through the following sub-categories:

- the mechanistic bureaucracy;[10]
- the professional bureaucracy.

The first of these variants of the bureaucracy is particularly rigid, while the second allows or even encourages individual initiative and judgement, albeit within limits that are usually clearly demarcated. This greater amount of freedom is related to the kind of work that the organisation performs, being normally more intellectually challenging for the majority of its personnel.

The most rigid versions of hierarchical organisations are hardly found in the development sphere. Still, *examples* of quite inflexible structures abound, most frequently in the government sphere but even among large NGOs and NGOs that limit themselves to highly specialised repetitive activities. Examples of such activities may be construction of a specific type of infrastructure (such as drilling and installation of tube wells) and certain kinds of relief work.

However, the large majority of NGOs – big and small – and even most development focusing government agencies may be most appropriately referred to as professional bureaucracies. This form is also typical for many research organisations.

THE LOOSELY-COUPLED NETWORK

The overall characterising *features* of this configuration are that it consists of people who primarily work together on a case-to-case basis, often through changing partnerships, and that the persons normally relate to each other on fairly equal terms.

---

[10]   This is referred to by Mintzberg (1983) as 'machine bureaucracy', directly reflecting key features of most manufacturing companies.

Commonly, administrative and operating tasks tend to blend into single efforts. However, relatively large and formalised organisations may have a permanent and stable administrative unit (falling under the category of 'support staff'), having arrangement of jobs, work scheduling, etc. as main duties. Usually, such organisations also have one person as their formalised manager. People may be employed in or work with these organisations on a permanent basis or more casually.

Loosely-coupled networks may be particularly *suitable* in unstable environments, that is, when opportunities or constraints may change quickly or may emerge and subside in an unpredictable manner. This form may also be appropriate when organisations have to innovate in order to survive or expand, whereby the kind of expertise that is needed may change or fluctuate.

In the development field, this form is *found* mainly in organisations that focus entirely or primarily on training, advisory services or research. Relief organisations and some other service organisations, whose mission may be to respond to natural or man-made calamities or address other unpredictable problems (such as disease outbreaks), may also be loosely-coupled networks. Additionally, some NGOs with a fairly general community-service purpose (being sometimes also community-based), may be structured in this way, relying on different people for different contributions to different activities that they undertake.

THE MATRIX

The main characterising *feature* of this form is that some or all persons in the organisation are responsible to two leaders (or hierarchy of leaders) for all or some of the work that they perform.

The matrix form may be seen as a construct for trying to blend major advantages of the hierarchy and the loosely-coupled network. More specifically, it is often resorted to for the *purpose* of combining stability and predictability in certain respects with innovativeness and flexibility in other respects.

For instance, a non-governmental organisation may be organised hierarchically for activities that are performed on a regular basis, such as agricultural demonstrations, vaccinations, or advocacy work in a particular field. Simultaneously, the organisation may want to explore the possibility of entering into a new field of activity or to undertake research on a particular topic that requires varied expertise, for which purpose it may recruit a manager and deploy selected persons from different sections of the organisation.

The last-mentioned persons will, then, be formally responsible to the team manager for the specific job to which they have been assigned, while being simultaneously more generally responsible to the head of the organisational sections to which they belong. In a few instances, though, the special assignment may be managed as a genuinely collective effort, without any formal manager for it; the responsibility for that job will then be shared by those involved.

A matrix organisation may also be made up of sections of two or more organisations or be interfaced with other organisations.

An example of this may be the planning and co-ordinating body of a comprehensive district development programme (often called Integrated Rural Development Programme – IRDP). That unit may consist of one leader, who may be the district head of a government department, and of district representatives of other government departments (and, possibly, other organisations). All or most of these people may then work partly with IRDP matters and partly with other line agency matters, with concomitant responsibility structures. Innovativeness and flexibility are normally greater in the IRDP sphere than in the line agency sphere, but this may vary.

4. ORGANISATIONAL CULTURE

The concept of 'organisational culture' has its roots in the anthropological concept of 'social culture'. In anthropology and related social sciences, the latter has been comprehensively used to denote relatively enduring sets of values and norms that underlie a social system along with core manifestations of these values and norms.

'Organisational culture' has become an important concept in organisation analysis and has been comprehensively explored in much management literature.[11]

Generally stated, an organisation's culture is *the set of values, norms and perceptions that frame and guide the behaviour of individuals in the organisation and the organisation as a whole, along with connected social and physical features (artefacts), constructed by the organisation's members, that are expressions of or may influence organisational behaviour.* All these facets of culture are usually strongly influenced by the history and customs of the society in which the organisation is located.

Values and norms that influence organisational performance may differ among the organisation's members. Influencing and unifying an organisation's culture is often one of the main leadership challenges.

Organisational *values* are closely linked to the organisation's vision and mission.[12] For an organisation to be able to pursue its mission consistently and with vigour, it is normally essential that the mission reflects the basic relevant values of the organisation's leaders, and usually also important that it conforms with dominant values among the membership of the organisation more broadly.

The concepts of mission and values may be even more important in development organisations than in many other organisations, and may constitute the very cornerstone in some of them, particularly organisations with a service mission whose members may not get much material reward for the work that they do.

Examples of important *norms* and *perceptions* may be: the extent of individualism or group conformity, attitudes to new ideas and proposals for change, loyalty vis-à-vis colleagues in work related

---

[11] For overviews and relatively broad discussions, see, for instance: Porras (1987), Burke (1992), Pugh and Hickson (1997) and, with more specific reference to development organisations, Cusworth and Franks (1993) and AIT (1998).

[12] For definitions of these concepts, see Chapter Two.

matters, concern for other members as human beings, the perception of customers or beneficiaries, and the perception of strains and rewards in one's work.

For instance, in a study of a community-based micro-finance programme in an Asian country, Dale (2000) considers the following features of culture to be particularly important for good performance and sustainability of the involved people's organisations:

- good knowledge by all the members about all common affairs;
- active participation by the members in common activities;
- respect for and adherence to agreed formal and informal rules of behaviour;
- sensitivity to special problems and needs of individual members;
- mutual trust and solidarity;
- a willingness to sacrifice for the common good.

Artefacts (relatively overt expressions) of an organisation's culture may be: rituals, formality of interpersonal communication, work stories, jargon, office layout, and formality of dress.

However, the behaviour of individuals in the organisation, even on clearly work-related matters, may not always reflect or even be considered to be part of the organisation's culture. It may often be more determined by the individuals' background and experiences outside the organisation. Whenever such externally induced behaviour conflicts with aspects of the organisation's prevailing culture, it may influence negatively the work environment of the organisation, depending on factors such as the amount of discord it represents with what others in the organisation consider as right or important, and how many persons display such conflicting behaviour.

A distinction has commonly been made between the three main organisational cultures of power, role and task.[13]

A *power culture* is often visualised as a spider's web, with the power concentrated with the 'spider' at the centre. There are few

---

[13]   These categories were introduced by Handy (1983).

rules, and decisions are made by and reflect the personal choice of the centrally placed individual or individuals.

In the *role culture*, the organisation rests on clearly defined sets of rules and tasks, in which posts (directly reflecting roles) are more important than the persons holding the posts. This is also referred to as 'bureaucratic culture'.

An organisation with a *task culture* has no single source of power and is not primarily governed by rules. It is geared towards fulfilling changing objectives through related sets of tasks. Expertise in specific fields is crucial, and teamwork is common.

The attentive reader will have noticed the close relationship between these culture categories and the organisational forms presented in the previous section. Each of the cultures and their structural manifestations have their advantages and disadvantages for development organisations, as stated in that chapter.

Moreover, these cultural features are inter-related with the mechanisms applied for co-ordinating an organisation's work, as will be elaborated in Section 8 of this chapter.

5. OTHER ORGANISATIONAL FEATURES

RULES

Rules are *general provisions for regulating the behaviour of individuals in the organisation and the organisation as a whole*, in internal matters and in dealings with outside bodies.

Rules are usually formalised to larger or lesser extents, i.e., explicitly stated in writing. Such formal rules are commonly referred to as 'procedures'. But rules may also be more informal; in such cases, they may be quite direct manifestations of the organisation's culture, and the distinction between rules and culture becomes blurred.

As mentioned, the degree to which the work of organisations (including development organisations) is regulated by rules varies greatly, being particularly much related to their form and culture.

ADMINISTRATIVE SYSTEMS

These encompass all *formally designed and established sets of routines that directly focus on co-ordinating and controlling the organisation's work.*

Main examples of administrative systems in most organisations beyond a minimum size are: information management systems (including monitoring systems), financial accounting systems, and personnel management systems.

The variety, importance and complexity of administrative systems vary greatly between development organisations. Besides their size, these may largely depend on their form (being, as we have seen, related to the degree of bureaucratisation). Other influencing factors may be their field of work, aspects of organisational culture and whether they are governmental, private or voluntary.

TECHNOLOGY

An organisation's technology encompasses *the set of tools at the organisation's disposal relating to the planning and implementation of its work, along with the knowledge in using the tools.*

For most development organisations, concepts, methods and techniques of planning their programmes or projects may be essential, as may be guidelines for implementing and monitoring the planned activities. More specific tools for converting inputs into outputs are also normally needed, examples of which may be a teaching methodology, techniques for organisation-building, and physical things such as hand tools, machines and energy.

INCENTIVES

These are the *rewards which the personnel or members of the organisation get from their work*, in terms of money, other tangible benefits, and intangible benefits (such as work satisfaction). Formalised reward mechanisms may be referred to as a reward system, which may be considered as one of the organisation's administrative systems.

Most organisations have some reward system. However, in many development organisations, non-formalised intangible rewards may be at least as important as the tangible ones and in some public benefit organisations even the only kind of reward, at least for some of the organisations' personnel.

6. MANAGEMENT AND LEADERSHIP

While the concepts of 'management' and 'leadership' may sound fluffy and are very difficult to define precisely, the notions involved are obviously crucial for the performance of organisations, including, of course, development organisations.

The two terms are sometimes used interchangeably or largely so; in other cases, management is considered as the wider concept, embedding leadership.

Thus, Mintzberg (1989) refers to the 'leader' role as only one among several 'management roles'. The *management roles* are seen as the responsibilities and related activities which the head or the heads of the organisation – i.e., the 'manager' or the group of 'managers'– need to take on and perform, in order to steer or guide the organisation well. The author specifies altogether ten management roles, which are grouped under three broader categories: the interpersonal, the informational, and the decisional.

As I consider this framework to convey dimensions of management particularly well, it is summarised below:

Interpersonal roles

Figurehead	Being a symbolic head, carrying out a number of routine duties of a legal or social nature;
Leader	Motivating and inspiring colleagues through the use of influence and guidance and the application of vision and judgement;
Liaison	Maintaining networks of formal and informal contact within and outside the organisation.

Informational roles

Monitor	Seeking and receiving information to understand the organisation and its environment;
Disseminator	Transmitting, inwards and outwards, factual information as well as information that involves interpretation and value judgements;
Spokesperson	Giving information to outsiders about the organisation's purpose, pursuits and achievements.

Decisional roles

Entrepreneur	Searching the organisation and its environment for strengths and opportunities and promoting related changes of the organisation;
Disturbance handler	Taking corrective action when the organisation faces disturbances (major conflicts or crises);
Resource allocator	Allocating the resources at the organisation's disposal;
Negotiator	Representing the organisation at major negotiations and making commitments of organisational resources.

Thus, according to Mintzberg, *leadership* is limited to motivational abilities and actions on the part of the manager.

Applying a broader perspective on *leadership,* AIT (1998) considers this concept to encompass:

- developing a clear vision of the future towards which the organisation's people can commit their energy;
- building a supportive organisational culture;
- enabling the people in the organisation to do good work;
- creating and responding to opportunities in the organisation's environment.

Leaders may emphasise various aspects differently and interact in different ways. A commonly used term for expressing a leader's perceptions and mode of interaction is *leadership style.*

Blake and Mouton,[14] referred to by Burke (1992), among many others, developed a 'leadership grid', the two dimensions of which are 'Concern for People' and 'Concern for Production'. The concern on each dimension may be assessed on an ordinal measurement scale (from very low to very high).

Leadership that is characterised by low concern on both dimensions is called 'impoverished management', as opposed to 'team management', reflecting high concern on the two dimensions. Leadership with high concern for people and low concern for production is termed 'country club management', and leadership with low concern for people and high concern for production is called 'authority compliance'.[15]

Farey (1993) presents a more elaborate framework, where he juxtaposes Blake and Mouton's dimension with the concepts of 'transformational' and 'transactional', corresponding to a distinction between 'leadership' and 'management'. Thus, on the one axis is 'Concern for Task' versus 'Concern for People', on the other axis 'Transformational' (emphasis on leadership) versus 'Transactional' (emphasis on management).

Main characterising features of a transformational (*leadership*) approach are future vision, risk-taking and innovativeness, while a transactional (*management*) approach places the main emphasis on productivity, problem-solving and correctness. Leadership/management behaviour is then expressed by terms such as 'charismatic' (highly transformational and high concern for people), 'mechanistic' (highly transactional and high concern for task), etc.[16]

---

[14] Blake, R.R. and Mouton, J.S. (1964): *The Managerial Grid;* Houston: Gulf.

[15] We immediately notice that Blake and Mouton, as well, give 'leadership' a much broader meaning than Mintzberg, referred to further above.

[16] For supplementing the sketchy presentation above, the reader may read the brief, yet instructive, overview by Analoui (1993) of changing perceptions of management skills.

Moreover, leadership may be analysed more directly in relation to the *needs of people* in the organisation. That is, how should a leader act in order to motivate and enable, as effectively as possible, people in the organisation to perform well? This is commonly referred to as 'coaching'. Obviously, what the approach should be depends on characteristics of the people to be coached.

According to Max Landsberg,[17] referred to in AIT (1998), it mainly depends on these persons' 'skill' (how able they are at doing a piece of work) and their 'will' (how confident and motivated they are to do it). Thus, people with low skill and low will need to be 'directed', those with low skill and high will should be 'guided', those with high skill and low will should be 'motivated', and people who have high skill and high will ought to get authority 'delegated' to them.

Beyond the relatively specific management and leadership aspects that are mentioned in the paragraphs above, main issues of management and leadership are in this book addressed or implied under other headings of the present chapter, notably in Sections 2, 3 and 4 (on organisational form and culture) and in Section 8 (on co-ordination).

7. WORK PROCESSES AND ROLE STRUCTURE

PROCESSES AND FUNCTIONS

Processes of work in organisations may be defined as *the interaction between units and individuals within the organisation and between the organisation and its environment, for the purpose of fulfilling the organisation's objectives.*

Processes relate to tasks and jobs (terms which we have already been using). The former mean *clearly specified and delimited pieces of work* by individuals or units in the organisation, while the latter stand for *clusters of closely related tasks.*

---

[17] Landsberg, M. (1996): *The Tao of Coaching;* London: Harper Collins.

A less precise term, <u>activity</u>, is often used with similar meaning as 'task' or 'job', or it may contain a notion of 'task' and 'process' combined.[18]

In strategic development planning, processes of work (which may then be referred to as planning processes) are interfaced with the strategy dimensions that address 'how'-questions, namely: blueprint – process, from above – from below, and excluding – participatory. In other words, the principles that are expressed by these sets of planning modes steer the processes of planning (that is, how planning is conducted).

A set of similar tasks is appropriately referred to as a work <u>category</u>. In development work, major task-sets have widely come to be termed <u>functions</u>.

In development work, one normally distinguishes between the following main functions:

Planning

A process of decision-making, of strategic and operational nature, in any combination of planning modes, encompassing:

- generation and processing of information;
- deciding on general aims and courses of action;

---

[18] Task and activities within a programme or project are normally related, to larger or lesser extent, to other tasks and activities within that programme or project. This is reflected in the term 'work breakdown structure', commonly used in operational (project) planning, in particular. With this is meant a breakdown of components of the programme or project into smaller and smaller units, the tasks of which become more and more closely related to each other.

For instance, an area development programme may consist of broad sector-components (such as agriculture development and road construction), each containing several projects. Each of the latter, in turn, may be broken further down into main work categories (such as management, design and construction), and then into even more narrow clusters of tasks.

For further elaboration and discussion, see, for instance, Rosenau (1992) and Cusworth and Franks (1993).

- specifying objectives, envisaged outputs, inputs, tasks and processes of work, organisational form, and other aspects of organisation.[19]

Implementation

Activities (work tasks and related processes) that transform inputs into outputs.[20]

Monitoring

Frequent largely routine-wise collection of, analysis of, and reporting on information about work performance; comparison of this with the programme or project plans; and any connected proposals for corrective action.

Evaluation

Compared with monitoring, a more thorough examination, at specified points in time, of organisations, programmes or projects, commonly with emphasis on impacts and additionally often on efficiency, effectiveness, relevance, sustainability and replicability.[21]

Operation

Continued organised use of a facility which has been created (such as an irrigation system) or continuation of an organised activity which has been introduced (such as improved agricultural extension).

Maintenance

Continued upkeep of facilities created or qualities established (such as a water supply system, a building, or a body of knowledge).

---

[19] Planning is examined in Chapter Three (the emphasis being on strategic planning).

[20] 'Inputs', 'outputs' and other terms that express components of means-ends chains of development work are specified and illustrated by examples in Chapter Three, Sections 6 and 7.

[21] On 'monitoring' and 'evaluation', see also footnote no. 1 of the present chapter.

In Chapter Six, the two concepts are clarified further, after which 'evaluation' is more comprehensively analysed.

ROLE STRUCTURE

Relations between tasks/jobs and actors (i.e., who do what) are a crucial issue in virtually any organisation and development programme and project.

Numerous techniques exist for visualising such role structures. They are usually referred to as charting and most of the resulting figures as charts or diagrams, although some may have tabular form. Such techniques are helpful tools for planning, co-ordinating and monitoring development work, commonly the more so the more complex the programme or project is.

It is not within the scope of this book to describe and analyse the range of such techniques and diagrams, as we are not much concerned with operational details. For further exploration of charting techniques, the reader is referred to other literature.[22]

I will here only illuminate aspects of role structure through two examples of relatively simple charts.

Figure 4.3, a generalised version of cases from my research, conveys a summary picture of the role structure in two similar agricultural projects in the same country, broken down by the main functions of planning, implementation and monitoring. Projects of this nature are ordinarily the responsibility of one department, in the figure referred to as the 'subject line agency'. In this case, the projects were undertaken within two regional development programmes with similar overall objectives and organisational set-up, having their own co-ordination apparatus as well as the authority to involve and deal with numerous government agencies, in particular.

---

[22] For development projects, a good overview of main techniques is found in Cusworth and Franks (1993). A more detailed presentation for projects is found in Rosenau (1992). Waters (1996) contains a thorough analysis of operations management, with emphasis on business companies, in which are incorporated numerous charting techniques that may be adjusted for use in development programmes and projects. For more simple presentations of one body of tools, process mapping, I refer to Galloway (1994) and Damelio (1996).

FIGURE 4.3

ROLE STRUCTURE BY FUNCTION AND LEVEL: AN EXAMPLE

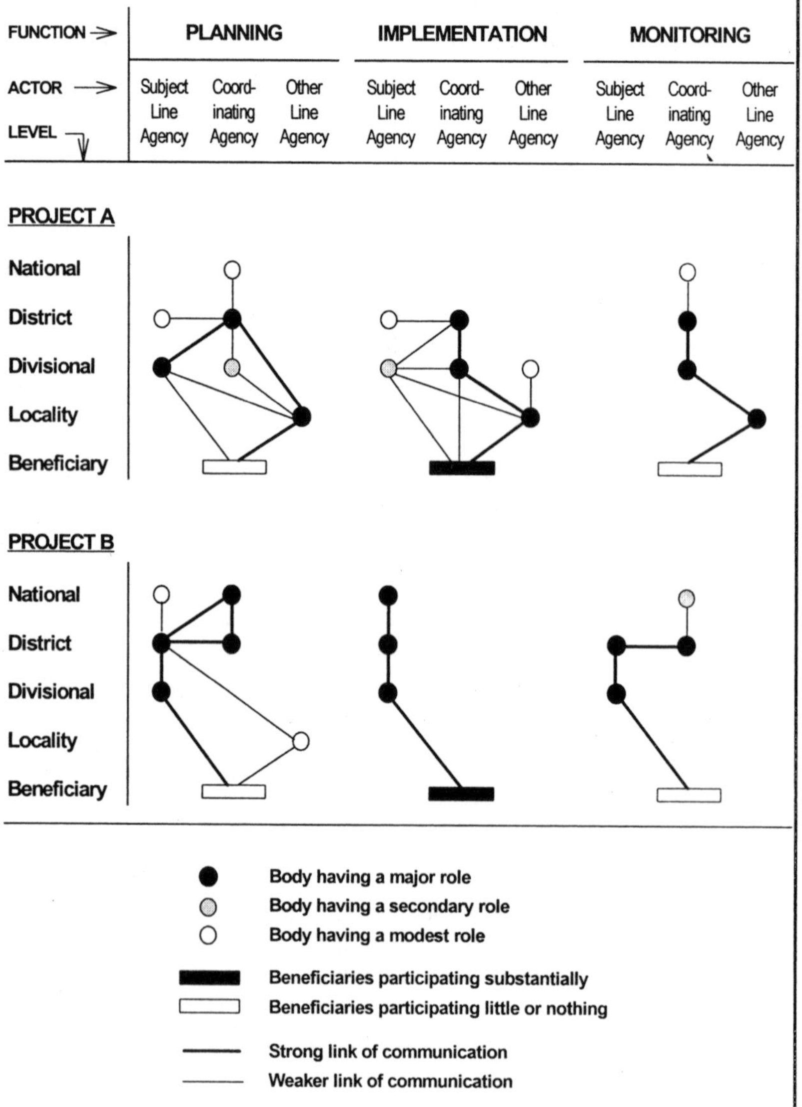

FUNCTION →	PLANNING			IMPLEMENTATION			MONITORING		
ACTOR →	Subject Line Agency	Coord- inating Agency	Other Line Agency	Subject Line Agency	Coord- inating Agency	Other Line Agency	Subject Line Agency	Coord- inating Agency	Other Line Agency

PROJECT A

National
District
Divisional
Locality
Beneficiary

PROJECT B

National
District
Divisional
Locality
Beneficiary

● Body having a major role
◉ Body having a secondary role
○ Body having a modest role

▬ Beneficiaries participating substantially
▭ Beneficiaries participating little or nothing

—— Strong link of communication
—— Weaker link of communication

TABLE 4.1

ROLE STRUCTURE BY ACTIVITY: AN EXAMPLE

	Organising training	Conducting training	Supplying materials	Construction (Facility A)	Construction (Facility B)	---
Department 1						---
Post A	S		S	S	S	
Post B			E			
Post C	E	A				
Department 2						---
Post A		S				
Post B		E				
Contractor					E	
Community organisation				E		---

E Execution   **S** Supervision   **A** Assistance

The different role structure reflects different strategies in the two projects, being, in turn, related to somewhat different missions and overall strategies of their parent programmes.

Most importantly, Project A aimed more at alleviating the poverty of households with little land than did Project B. In strategy terms used in this book, Project A was more normative. It was, in addition, planned more from below, with more farmer involvement, than Project B. These strategy choices of Project A were seen by the programme authorities as requiring comprehensive involvement also by other government bodies than the subject line agency, since farmers with little land would normally not be targeted by that agency. It resulted in an organisationally quite complex project with high demands on co-ordination. Project B was, in comparison, a more conventional line agency scheme, with only limited need for co-ordination between agencies and between these and the farmers.

Table 4.1 illustrates the role structure in selected activities of implementation of an imagined project. Unlike in Figure 4.3, the roles are broken down by the mode of involvement, i.e., whether the respective bodies have executing, supervisory or advisory responsibility. These additional pieces of information might, however, have been provided in the figure also.

For comparative presentation of the role structure of two or more programmes or projects, the figure is clearly the superior tool.

8. CO-ORDINATION OF DEVELOPMENT WORK

Structuring work relations between units and individuals is a major challenge of organisations, the more so the bigger and more complex they are and the more outward connections they have. Development organisations are no exception in this respect.

The term 'co-ordination' expresses well this basic endeavour of connecting and synchronising work tasks within organisations, programmes and projects. Well operationalised, the concept may be elaborated into an effective tool for managing organisations and the work that they do and for analysing their performance.

Somewhat more concisely, while still at a general level, I will define <u>co-ordination</u> as *harmonisation of the work done by different bodies within an organisation or by collaborating organisations, through specific mechanisms that are effectuated through specific tasks, being usually the full or main responsibility of specific units or persons within the organisation or organisations.*

Mintzberg (1983) elaborates a set of basic co-ordination mechanisms which, he demonstrates, tend to correspond with several other organisational features and are particularly closely intertwined with the form of organisations.[23]

---

[23]   The co-ordination mechanisms specified by Mintzberg are: direct supervision, standardisation of work processes, standardisation of worker skills, standardisation of work outputs, and mutual adjustment. Any organisation, he argues, will use some such mechanism for co-ordinating its pursuits.

Drawing on Mintzberg's analysis as well as some earlier work of mine (Dale [1992]), I present below a set of co-ordination mechanisms that I consider to be a widely applicable framework for analysing co-ordination in development programmes and projects.

Promoting a common vision

An organisation's vision has earlier (in Chapter Two) been defined as the perception of a future situation that the organisation aims to help create. It is closely related to organisational values and may, for that reason, be a particularly important concept for development organisations.

If unambiguously shared by the organisation's members, or by the members of co-operating organisations, the vision may be a strong motivating agent and a 'guiding star' that pulls the activities of the members in the same direction. It may also represent a main inducement for people in some organisations to continue their work in spite of no or little material remuneration.

By the same logic, efforts at building a common vision may have a harmonising and synchronising effect on the work of an organisation or interconnected work of two or more organisations.

In the development sphere, this co-ordination mechanism tends to be particularly important in organisations with clear and broadly shared images of their pursuits, provided that the staff or members are also well informed about the results of the organisation's work at large.

Grouping organisations by their structure into five main types, termed 'structural configurations', he then endeavours to show that each configuration depends on one primary co-ordination mechanism: the 'simple structure' relies mainly on direct supervision; the 'machine bureaucracy' on standardisation of work processes; the 'professional bureaucracy' on standardisation of skills; the 'divisionalised form' on standardisation of outputs; and the 'adhocracy' on mutual adjustment.

While common features exist, the reader will notice some differences between Mintzberg's structure classification and our classification of development organisations by their form, undertaken in Section 2 of the present chapter.

This combination characterises many collectives, in which, therefore, this mechanism tends to be very important. It may also be important in many one-leader organisations, in which the personnel work in the spirit of their leader.

Establishing common objectives

In order to perform a clearly identifiable development role, a development organisation needs to clarify a mission (see Chapter Two) that harmonises with its vision, and, as more specific statements of intent, objectives for the work that it intends to undertake.

General objectives may apply to its whole development endeavour, while more specific objectives are required for specific parts of it (for instance, individual projects within a broader portfolio of projects). Co-operating organisations will, normally, also have to set common objectives for the development work that each of them contributes to (see Chapter Three, Section 7 for an example).

Clear objectives that carry the same meaning for everybody may be important for focusing the members' contributions. They are, usually, particularly important when units or individuals are granted substantial amounts of independence in their work, that is, when more directly regulating co-ordination mechanisms (see below) are not applied or are so to only limited extents. It may also be essential for work efficiency that all the people in the organisation or organisations agree on the objectives and feel a common commitment to them.

In order to achieve a broad commitment, leaders of development organisations should usually involve as large sections of their organisations as possible in discussing and agreeing on objectives. For development schemes in which one endeavours to get participation by beneficiaries or other stakeholders outside the directly responsible organisation or organisations, the performance may be substantially enhanced by involving these stakeholders as well in the specification of objectives.

Standardising outputs

By standardising the commodity or service that is produced, the organisation takes a big further step in co-ordinating its pursuit.

This has become a very common co-ordination mechanism in the business world. The idea is that, as long as the output is of specified quality (and, usually, quantity and price), it is not of major concern for the top management how the commodity or service is produced. In particular, this enables companies to multiply their production of identical commodities through subsidiary enterprises without having their top managers enmeshed in details of processes of work in each place.

In the development field, standardisation of outputs is less common. It is primarily resorted to in programmes that involve construction of the same kind of facilities (such as school buildings, latrines or fishing boats) in many places by different organisations or individuals. The concern is then to ensure that the constructed facilities are of the same design, quality and cost, while, simultaneously, the programme managers may allow the implementing agencies substantial freedom in undertaking the work.

This co-ordination mechanism may be made operational through a combination of: providing the implementers with standard drawings, bills of quantities, cost details, and any other specifications; controlling that the standards are complied with; and making funding subject to such compliance.

This mechanism is, generally, much more applicable in development work with a clearly functional perspective than in programmes with normative planning, as the latter will normally open up for a broader and more varied set of activities and outputs.

Since standardisation of outputs normally needs bureaucratic control, it is, in the development field, primarily resorted to by typically hierarchical organisations.

Standardising skills

By standardisation of skills, in one organisation or within similar or co-operating organisations, is meant a conscientious effort to ensure that people who are to undertake identical or similar tasks have the same qualifications for doing the work, assuming that this will result in work of the same quality, undertaken with similar efficiency.

This may be done in two main ways: by recruiting people who have the same skills, or by training people who are already in place to obtain the same skills. Such training may be given in many forms: as conventional classroom training, through workshops, by formalised on-the-job training, and through informal facilitation.

Standardising skills may be a mechanism for co-ordinating work in most kinds of organisations, including development organisations. It is widely resorted to in development programmes and projects involving tasks that are to be replicated by more than one person. The persons undertaking the work may belong to the same organisation, may be members of different organisations, or may even be individual implementers, such as farmers.

Skill standardisation is commonly closely related to specialisation, in that it may help ensure complementarity of a range of specialised skills, required in organisations that perform complex jobs. This may be particularly important in bureaucratic organisations and commonly even more so in loosely-coupled networks, in which team-work dominates.

For example, ensuring a set of standardised skills of complementary nature is commonly the main mechanism of co-ordinating the contributions of individuals in a consultancy company (being commonly a loosely-coupled network). Here, this mechanism will, normally, be coupled with the establishment of common objectives for each job and mutual adjustment among the persons who are involved in the same job.

Routinising work

This mechanism, which may also be termed 'standardisation of work processes', is a more direct steering tool of the work of organisations than any of the mechanisms presented above.

Routinisation may often be essential to ensure both high work efficiency and a required degree of standardisation of the outputs. Routines may be more or less standardised across organisations, programmes or projects (such as basic routines of accounting) or they may be tailored for individual organisations or schemes.

This strong mechanism of co-ordination is a characterising feature of what we have called mechanistic bureaucracies. Moreover, in such hierarchical organisations, the need to routinise tends to increase with increasing size and complexity of the organisation.

Development organisations also resort to routinisation, largely depending on their form, the character of their work, and sometimes their size and complexity.

Commonly, organisations or units within them which undertake work of a functional nature may routinise more of the work than organisations or units which work in a more normative mode, because most tasks may be more pre-determined with the former mode. Closely related, routinisation is normally feasible to a larger extent in development schemes that are planned in a blueprint mode than in programmes with process planning.

Direct supervision

Direct supervision means that one unit or person in the organisation directly oversees the work of others. It usually involves both instruction and control, in various combinations. In some instances, however, the control function may be performed largely separately, as in programmes and projects that are monitored by a special monitoring unit.

Direct supervision may be perceived as the most direct form of co-ordination. Commonly, it has tended to be seen as the most effective form as well, particularly in small organisations and in relatively small units within bigger ones, in which the supervisor will have good overview of the work that is done.

Direct supervision is a main characterising feature of the one-leader body, where it is done by the leader him- or herself or partly delegated to some personal assistant(s) or deputy leader(s). But some control function, at least, will be instituted in any development organisation which uses financial resources that are to be accounted for, internally or externally (being almost always the case). Thus, some degree of direct supervision is applied in virtually all development programmes and projects.

Mutual adjustment

With mutual adjustment is meant co-ordination of work through informal communication between the involved bodies. By this feature of informality, it distinguishes itself from all the other co-ordination mechanisms. And by its invitation to lateral (as opposed to vertical, top-down) communication, it is the anti-thesis of direct supervision.

Mutual adjustment is usually the most important mechanism of co-ordination in collective organisations, such as local community-based groups of various kinds. It is also needed for making organisations with a matrix form perform well. The mechanism may also be highly important in loosely-coupled organisations, and may sometimes be resorted to as a supplementary mechanism even in hierarchical organisations or parts of them.

Except in some highly informal groups, mutual adjustment will be used in combination with some other mechanism or mechanisms. For instance, community organisations with an empowerment agenda will normally also emphasise promotion of a common vision, while other community organisations (such as savings and credit groups) may resort to substantial routinisation, usually in addition to both promotion of a common vision and mutual adjustment.

Table 4.2 summarises relations between organisational form and co-ordination mechanisms. The table visualises general tendencies, and larger or smaller deviations from this picture are not uncommon.

A couple of supplementary comments are:

We see that *hierarchical organisations* tend to apply the widest array of co-ordination mechanisms. This is due to their complex physical set-up in combination with the highly circumscribed nature of the tasks and jobs they undertake.

The many co-ordination mechanisms shown for *collective organisations* warrant an explanation. Besides mutual adjustment, being important for all collectives, the range of mechanisms largely reflects alternative options more than complementary measures, depending on the organisations' mission, size, etc. This was briefly exemplified under 'mutual adjustment' above.

TABLE 4.2
RELATION BETWEEN ORGANISATIONAL FORM
AND CO-ORDINATION MECHANISMS

CO-ORDINATION MECHANISM \ ORGANISATIONAL FORM	The Collective	The One-Leader Body	The Hierarchy	The Loosely-Coupled Network	The Matrix
Promoting a common vision	a	a			
Establishing common objectives	a	a	a	a	
Standardising outputs			a		
Standardising skills			a	M	a
Routinising work	a		M		a
Direct supervision		M	a		a
Mutual adjustment	M			a	M

M   Usually main co-ordination mechanism

a   Common additional co-ordination mechanism

Presenting a general tendency-pattern for *matrix organisations* (or matrix sub-entities of organisations) is particularly difficult and will not reflect all cases well. The four mechanisms of mutual adjustment, direct supervision, standardising skills and routinising work tend to be the main mechanisms required with this form. But which of them will be most important and whether all of them will be significant will vary.

Moreover, the mechanisms may differ substantially between the two axes of the matrix. The pattern shown may, commonly, be most typical for the most innovative set of activities, while reflecting poorly the other set.

Using the NGO case given in our presentation of 'The Matrix' in Section 2 as an example, the pattern that is presented in Table 4.2 (with 'mutual adjustment' as the main co-ordination mechanism) may be most directly applicable for the exploratory and research pursuits of the NGO, while the more conventional line pursuits may be co-ordinated differently.

In addition, however, harmonising the two (the exploratory and the more conventional pursuits respectively) will in itself require some amount of mutual adjustment.

All in all, therefore, mutual adjustment is considered as the most typical and, frequently, most important co-ordination mechanism of matrix organisations.

Analyses of co-ordination may be further refined by exploring the *tasks* by which the various co-ordination mechanisms have been, are being or may be executed. This may be done through a matrix of mechanisms and tasks, as exemplified in Table 4.3.

This table shows the mechanisms of co-ordination applied in a multi-sector programme with process planning, studied by me a few years ago.[24]

In such complex programmes, co-ordination is particularly challenging and may require many measures, as in this case. Most other programmes and projects would display a much simpler pattern.

Table 4.3 shows co-ordination as effectuated by the overall planning and monitoring body of the programme, which in this case was a sub-unit of a planning ministry at the district level. Thus, co-ordination in the programme was even more complex than shown, since many co-ordination requirements were taken care of by other bodies, primarily a number of government line departments and people's organisations.

---

[24]   A further analysis is made in Dale (1992). It should be noted, though, that the set of mechanisms and the terms of some tasks have been modified.

TABLE 4.3

CO-ORDINATION MECHANISMS AND TASKS: AN EXAMPLE

MECHANISMS \ TASKS	Conscientisation	Management training	Vocational training	Framework planning	Guidance in project planning	Project approval	Review meetings	Field visits	Progress report assessment	Sanctioning of payments
Promoting a common vision	●			●			○			
Establishing common objectives				●	○		○			
Standardising outputs			○							
Standardising skills		○	○		○					
Routinising work		○			○					
Direct supervision				●	○	●	●	○	●	●
Mutual adjustment				●			●	○		

● Strong co-ordination   ○ Some co-ordination

The study on which Table 4.3 is based substantiates the key role of co-ordination in development work and the fruitfulness of analysing organisation of such work in the perspective of co-ordination.

An overall conclusion of the study is that the set of co-ordination mechanisms and tasks differed substantially between, on the one hand, the programme illustrated here and, on the other hand, similar programmes with the same overall objectives, implemented simultaneously in the same country. A further major conclusion is that these differences were related to differences in more specific objectives and various strategy features. It is also argued that there were different degrees of compatibility (fit) between, on the one side, such objectives and features and, on the other side, the mechanisms of co-ordination applied. That is, the instituted means of co-ordination were more or less appropriate in their context.

This chapter has covered a wide range of topics and issues of organisation, being essential for designing and managing development work. Drawing on a broad range of literature on organisation and management – from the spheres of business, public administration and development – as well as on personal experience with development work, I have endeavoured to apply perspectives and formulate frameworks of direct applicability for development organisations and their pursuits. A related set of issues pertain to the building of such organisations. These will be addressed next, within a broader context of capacity-building. To this will be connected perspectives on participation and empowerment.

Chapter Five

PARTICIPATION, EMPOWERMENT AND CAPACITY-BUILDING

1. SCOPE AND BROAD DEFINITIONS

Involvement of people and augmentation of abilities of individuals and various societal entities are crucial dimensions of much development work. The corresponding concepts of 'participation', 'empowerment' and 'capacity-building' have come to be much emphasised in the development discourse over the last couple of decades. There are two main reasons for that: (a) increased stress among development agencies on 'good governance' and (b) widespread disappointment with long-term impacts of much development work, which has often been largely attributed to a technical emphasis and a delivery attitude in such work.

Participation, empowerment and capacity-building are commonly seen as *means* for creating sustained benefits of development efforts. Additionally, active involvement by citizens in societal affairs, more equal opportunities for various groups of people, and abilities of various kinds are now widely considered as development *ends* as well, that is, as desirable attributes of individuals and societal units in their own right.

The three concepts of 'participation', 'capacity-building' and 'empowerment' are inter-related and partly inter-dependent.

Participation is most often taken to mean involvement by 'common' people (i.e., by non-professionals) in various types and stages of development work. Frequently, these people are intended beneficiaries of the work that is undertaken. When that is the case, one commonly refers to the involvement as 'people's participation'. But 'participation' may also denote involvement by a range of other stakeholders with different interests and abilities.[1]

Capacity-building may apply to individuals, organisations, and various systems for regulating and managing societal affairs. Participation, in some sense, is normally required for capacities of any kind to be augmented.

By *empowerment* is basically meant a process whereby people acquire more influence over factors that shape their lives. The concept tends to be primarily applied for disadvantaged groups of people, and is usually linked to a vision of more equal living conditions in the society.

2. DIMENSIONS OF PARTICIPATION

PRINCIPLES OF PARTICIPATION

'Participation' has been used in different ideological contexts and has been given a variety of more specific meanings than indicated above, in development literature and among development organisations, planners and managers.

Any planned participatory development process, if well conceived and conscientiously designed and implemented, should be founded on some major tenets of development. While most of these may have fairly universal applicability, more specific justifications for participation may be used and may be warranted in specific situations.

---

[1]   In the sphere of planning, such perspectives were clarified further in the section on stakeholder analysis in Chapter Three and by the strategy concepts 'from above – from below' and 'excluding – participatory' in the same chapter.

Most fundamentally, as stated by Keough (1998), participatory development should be considered as 'at heart a philosophy', embedding the belief that 'it is the right way to conduct oneself with other human beings' (1998: 194).

This may, at times, conflict with ideas of work efficiency that development agencies have and also with methods and techniques that professionals have been trained in for planning, implementing, monitoring and evaluating development work.

One main principle about which there should be no major dispute, also emphasised by Keough (1998), is profound *respect* for other people. This is closely connected to *humility* regarding individual persons' perception about factors that contribute to shape their own lives, regarding development priorities that different people may have, and regarding knowledge and skills that participants may possess.

Underlying this principle is also the practical consideration that people may be reluctant to share their knowledge and to contribute comprehensively or constructively if they do not sense such respect and humility from planners, facilitators, managers and other persons in key positions.

Planners and managers of participatory development should also recognise the significance and potential of *local knowledge* for development pursuits in the respective local environments. Standardised knowledge that tends to be carried by professional development workers may be both superior in certain senses and adequate in many local contexts. Still, the additional and more specific knowledge that local residents have about their own environment may often enhance the relevance, effects and sustainability of development work.

Sometimes, local knowledge may conflict with that of professionals from outside, in which cases the situation and any development initiatives should be thoroughly discussed among the persons and agencies involved and choices of action arrived at which the local people believe in.

Theories about development and its management that planners, administrators and other practitioners may carry with them will be, at best, simplified approximations of real-world situations. Usually, therefore, development agencies ought to work in a basically *inductive* mode. That is, the starting point for their analysis and actions should be relevant aspects of the reality in specific work situations more than their general ideas (whether relating to the society or to development work). In order to generate the necessary information, contributions from others are usually required, and communication between stakeholders needs to be promoted.

One of the most difficult lessons to learn for development agencies which want to develop a commitment to participation is to *embrace uncertainty* in planning. Concrete and unambiguous answers are unusual in most development work. In participatory processes, uncertainty is normally increased through the variety of knowledge, perceptions and interests that the participants will usually have. Being able to relate to and deal constructively with issues for which many interpretations and choices exist is, therefore, essential in participatory development work.

This amplifies conceptions of uncertainty that were addressed in our discussion of strategy formulation, in Chapter Three. The reader may remember that strategic choices were conceived as decisions taken with main consideration given to uncertainties in the planning environment, and that such uncertainties were stated to be the basic rationale for 'incremental' or 'process' planning. Directly connected, uncertainties are basic to the concept of 'threat', being one of the main analytical categories of strategic planning.

The additional argument here, then, is that the amount of uncertainty tends to increase with broad participation in planning, because decisions may depend on difficult mediation between needs and interests of various stakeholders.

Moreover, if the planned work is to be implemented in a highly participatory mode as well, an additional amount of uncertainty may be induced about generation of the intended outputs, through greater management challenges during implementation.

MODES, PURPOSES AND CONDITIONALITIES
OF PARTICIPATION

Following Oakley et al. (1991), I will distinguish between three broad interpretations of 'participation' in the development field:

Participation as contribution

This is contribution to programmes and projects that are being or have been planned by others, on terms that those others have determined or at least framed. The contribution may be entirely free, induced or even enforced. It may be in the form of ideas, judgements, money, materials, or unpaid or lowly paid labour.

This has been the dominant perspective on participation in most development work, particularly in programmes and projects financed by government agencies.

Participation as organising

The idea is that people may be involved in development work more effectively if they are organised in some way. It is assumed that the participants have at least some influence over affairs of the organisations to which they belong, and one expects that resources may therewith be pooled and better managed.

The organisations may be externally conceived and introduced (for instance, many co-operatives and irrigation management committees), may be formed by people themselves, or may be developed through a combination of external and internal initiatives and contributions. People may sometimes organise in reaction to an external intervention, in order to protect or promote their interests. In other instances, people's organisations may emerge during a process of participation, which may initially have been driven from outside the local community or by other agents in the community.

Participation as empowering

Organisation may be seen as a means of empowerment and is often crucial for it. But, by implication of the notion of empowerment, the organisational activities must then be people-centred. Processes of empowerment may still be facilitated by or may even require communication with and support from outsiders, and a range of options for such communication and support exists. However, the communication must be in dialogue form, by which outside development organisations and workers emphasise soft inducement, information exchange and response rather than dictate and persuasion.[2]

Another basic feature of empowerment is that it brings to the surface conflicts of perception and interest, which need to be addressed conscientiously and systematically, but which can hardly ever be resolved through any standard set of actions.

The above links to a distinction between participation as a *means* and participation as an *end* of development. Or, in more nuanced terms, participation may be seen as located at lower or higher levels in means-ends chains of development.[3] Generally speaking, participation as contribution is a means and participation as empowering is a high-level end, while participation as organising may be either a means or an end, at some level, depending on the perspective applied.

Participation may occur in different <u>functions</u> and <u>tasks</u> of development programmes and projects, i.e., in problem and needs analysis, plan formulation, implementation, monitoring, evaluation, operation and/or maintenance.[4]

Participation in planning was in Chapter Three linked to one of the specified planning modes, namely, 'participatory' planning. If, in addition, the participating persons are common people in the respective community or organisation or they are direct representatives of such people, planning would be 'from below' as well, to a larger or lesser extent.

---

[2]   For a presentation and discussion of modes and issues of communication for development, see Servaes et al. (1996).

[3]   For a presentation of means-ends chains or hierarchies, see Chapter Three. We will also revert to them later in this chapter and in Chapter Six.

[4]   For definitions of these terms, see Chapter Four.

Participation as *empowering* usually occurs mainly in problem analysis and plan formulation, particularly at the stage of strategic planning, since it is at this stage that problems to be addressed are primarily analysed and main courses of action are decided on. In planning, empowerment may be achieved in one of two senses, or in a combination of the two. First, it may materialise through the influence that the participating people may exert on the kinds and magnitude of *benefits* for themselves from the development work that is planned. Second, it may materialise through the analytical *skills* that the participants may obtain from the processes of analysis and decision-making they are involved in.

Additionally, participation in monitoring and, particularly, evaluation may be empowering, especially when the information that is generated through these activities is fed back into planning, i.e., when it is utilised for re-examining and, possibly, modifying or supplementing work that has been done.[5]

Participation as *contribution* may occur primarily in the implementation of programmes and projects or in the operation and maintenance of facilities created. But contributions, in terms of people's ideas or opinions, may also be sought in the planning phase, as inputs into decision-making by others. The latter may be referred to as 'consultation'.

Organisation may be a means to make participation more effective in any of the mentioned functions. For instance, planning committees may be created for problem analysis and proposal generation, implementation may be done by promoted enterprises, and maintenance may be undertaken by established user groups.

There are several additional dimensions on which participation may be classified and analysed.

---

[5] Evaluations which aim at providing information for further planning and implementation in the same organisation, programme or project or for planning a directly connected programme or project may be referred to as *formative evaluations.* For a further discussion of them, see Chapter Six. That chapter also contains a section on *empowerment evaluation.*

Uphoff et al. (1979) present a simple and well-known framework for analysing participation in rural development. The authors broadly distinguish between three perspectives: participation *in what*, *who* participate, and *how* the participants are involved.

The 'in what' perspective broadly complies with our presentation above of participation by function (in planning, implementation, operation, monitoring or evaluation).[6]

'Who' participate (or may do so) depends, of course, on the kind of development effort and a range of other factors. In many community development programmes, for instance, a broad distinction may be made between residents, local leaders, government personnel and foreign personnel.

The 'how' perspective is the most challenging one and may invite specification of a range of sub-perspectives, depending on the organisation, programme or project studied and the emphasis and depth of the analysis. Uphoff et al. distinguish between the basis of participation (in terms of impetus and incentives), the forms of participation (basically the organisation of it), the extent of participation (i.e., the range of activities and the time used), and the effects of participation (in terms of lasting involvement and empowerment).

Dusseldorp (1981) lists a number of similar perspectives, in terms of several dimensions of participation. Each dimension is presented by opposite categories, which in reality constitute the endpoints of a continuum on the respective dimension. Slightly modified, the main dimensions of his framework are:

Free – Forced

This captures the extent to which participation occurs through one's free will or is forced, by law or by prevailing societal conditions.

---

[6]   Uphoff et al. (1979) also incorporate 'participation in benefits (or harmful consequences)'. I consider generation of benefits to be a too different aspect, both conceptually and in terms of the methods needed to study it, for this to be considered as a dimension of participation.

Spontaneous – Induced

Under the broad category of 'free', persons may start to participate entirely through their own conviction that it is appropriate or useful, or after they have been motivated by others to do so.

Direct – Indirect

In direct participation, the persons will involve themselves in an activity, such as attend a meeting or contribute labour; in indirect participation, they will be represented by some other person(s).

Complete – Partial

This denotes whether participation occurs in all main functions or stages of a development programme or project or in only one or some of them.

Intensive – Extensive

This expresses how regularly or frequently the participation occurs.

Additionally, Dusseldorp classifies participation by its effectiveness, by who are involved (corresponding to that dimension in Uphoff et al., just mentioned), and by its spatial and social spheres.

As already stated, we need to be conscious that broad participation usually increases the complexity of development work. In this perspective, the question of direct versus indirect participation is often crucial.

For development programmes and projects, this tends to be a particularly important choice at the stage of planning (including decision-taking).

More generally, direct versus indirect participation is a core question relating to local governance (the character of local governments and related systems of decision-making and organisation of local development work).

Closely connected is the question of the modalities of indirect participation. This is of great importance for many development organisations, programmes and projects, but it has most comprehensive implications for the functioning of governments, at both the central and local levels.

BOX 5.1

STRENGTHENING LOCAL GOVERNANCE: AN EXAMPLE

The country referred to here has had a highly centralised system of governance. Assisted by international donor agencies, efforts are underway to decentralise development work. One aspect of this is to build the capacity of embryonic self-governance institutions at the local level and to devise a procedure of local-level planning that balances work efficiency and replicability[7] with as broad participation of people as possible.

A part of the strategy is to provide initial training on decentralisation policy and decentralised planning and management to government agencies at the district level and to the presently rudimentary local governance body (LGB) at the local level.

This is intended to be followed by participatory processes in the local communities of need identification, problem analysis and proposal generation. Originally, a highly intensive approach was tried out, with a four-day exercise in participatory learning and action (PLA) in each village within the local government area (commonly encompassing 10–15 villages). However, these processes were found to take too much time to be replicable on any big scale. Therefore, a revised approach has been proposed, as follows:

- the PLA exercise to be scaled down to one workshop in each local government area, with participation by the present LGB, the few central government personnel at the local level, and one or two additional representatives from each village, to be chosen by the villagers;

- inducements to select female participants, as well, for the PLA workshop, and promotion of active involvement by non-LGB representatives and women in that workshop, through effective facilitation;

---

[7]　For clarification of these terms, see Chapter Six.

- continued facilitation and follow-up by the trainers at the subsequent stages of operational planning and implementation;
- a participatory evaluation towards the end of the first year's work programme, with the same set of actors as for the initial planning event.

It is recognised that this arrangement will be less effective in terms of promoting broad participation than village-based PLA workshops. On the other hand, it will be less time-consuming and in better conformity with the limited capacity for training. It may also be more easily replicated during subsequent annual rounds of planning, with less assistance from outside.

Linked to the issues addressed above, primarily relating to planning, are abilities and arrangements for implementation and financial management, not further addressed here.

Local governments, as normally defined, are supposed to be representative bodies. Simultaneously, as mentioned in Chapter Two, over large parts of the less developed world they tend, for various reasons, not to be perceived as genuinely representative of the majority, or certain sections, of the population within their geographical areas of authority.

This has led to various initiatives to involve the population at large, or marginalised groups within it, more directly in problem analysis, idea generation and prioritisation. Most such efforts have probably been made within some donor-supported programmes of community development and local-level institution-building.[8]

An example of issues involved and how they may be addressed is given in Box 5.1. The arrangements proposed are those of a group of consultants, including myself. At the level of generality presented here, they have in principle been accepted by the national government.

---

[8] 'Institution-building' will be defined shortly.

The views that have been presented in this section may be broadly referred to as an *action oriented* or *interactionist* perspective on participation. As stated by Pongquan (1992), this has become the dominant perspective in studies of participation (and, indeed, development management more broadly). This perspective emphasises interests of various stakeholders, inter-personal relations and negotiations, and processes by which decisions are arrived at and followed up.

It must be stressed that formal rules and a formalised institutional framework are important as well, and should be incorporated into most studies of participation, along with analysis of actions and interactions.

The <u>arguments for participation</u> vary with the scope of the latter.

When considered as a high level *end* of development (i.e., as empowering), the basic argument is, by implication, injustices in the society which need to be combated through empowerment of those who are disadvantaged.

As stated earlier, 'participation as empowering' and 'participation as organising' are often closely related. By the same logic, *empowering participation* may link on to 'organisation-building', as this term will be defined shortly. It may also link, more comprehensively, to the broader concept of 'institution-building', as this will be defined. With the latter is basically meant that the thrust may involve more than forming some organisation of deprived people for doing development work for their own benefit. It may, additionally, aim at creating abilities of non-organisational nature on the part of the people thus organised to challenge existing structures and other constraints that inhibit improvements in their lives.

As already alluded to, not all notions of organisation-building incorporate empowerment. Such more narrow conceptions are commonly found even in development work which involves organisation of clearly deprived people. In such instances, one may say that functional perspectives prevail in contexts that would call for a more normative approach.

When seen more as a *means* (i.e., as contribution and sometimes even as organising), a whole range of arguments for participation have been presented by various authors, including:

- making reliable information more easily accessible for planners;
- increasing the number of people who may benefit from a programme or project;
- making use of local technical knowledge;
- adapting design and organisation of programmes and projects to fit local conditions;
- reduced cost for the government in the implementation of development work and the provision of services;
- improved utilisation and maintenance of facilities.[9]

Participation may occur at different geographical levels, but most forms of participation may materialise wholly or mainly in the persons' immediate environment, i.e., within the persons' local community.[10]

Thus, empowering participation involves, primarily, increased influence over factors in the participating persons' local environment. Organisation of the disadvantaged people at the community level is, usually, crucial for achieving this. In the sphere of planning, this involves planning from below.

However, to yield substantial benefits, participation at the community level usually needs to occur within an enabling wider environment. Examples of important external factors may be: national policies and laws; administrative effectiveness and efficiency in government agencies (at various levels); support by a wider network of people's organisations (within a region or a country); support by international, national or regional non-governmental organisations;

---

[9] See also, for instance, Oakley et al. (1991) and Uphoff (1986).

[10] Participation may occur at different levels within organisations as well. Main issues and arguments relating to organisational and geographical levels are similar.

and various kinds of infrastructure linking the local community to centres and other areas.

In other words, participation at the local level is conditioned by numerous <u>influencing factors</u> both in the local community itself and in the wider environment.[11]

Common factors that may <u>constrain</u> participation are:

- the *political environment*, at the national level and/or lower levels, in terms of oppression by the political and legal system or dominance of individual politicians;

- *power structures* in local communities (for instance, between people who possess much and little land or between political sections);

- *conservative attitudes* (for instance, traditional views on participation by women);

- *little awareness* among people of rights they may have or opportunities they may exploit;

- *administrative obstacles* in government agencies (such as requirements of written documentation and cumbersome routines for processing information and making decisions);

- emphasis on *standardisation* and *quantification* of targets and benefits in development programmes and projects, which tends to leave out issues relating to participation (such as changes in self-confidence or different aspects of empowerment);

- *rigid professionalism* (or 'normal professionalism', in the terminology of Chambers [1993]) among development and service officials (for instance, in the agricultural extension and formal health services);

- a *didactic (lecturing) style of teaching* by officials and development workers.[12]

---

[11] For a good discussion of factors influencing participation, see, in addition to books already mentioned, Burkey (1993).

[12] Most of these factors are mentioned and further discussed in Cohen (1996).

TOOLS FOR PROMOTING PARTICIPATION

An additional aspect pertaining to participation in development work is the methods and techniques that may be used in participatory inquiry, planning, implementation, monitoring and evaluation. A substantial exploration of that comprehensive, while relatively technical, topic would lead us beyond the scope of this book. A few brief reflections will have to suffice, pertaining mainly to planning and evaluation.

A main distinction may be warranted between mechanisms of participation (a) within development organisations and (b) in the locations of the development work, such as local communities.

On the planning side, participatory analysis by an *organisation's personnel* may involve going through jointly some or all of the steps of strategic planning, as presented in Chapter Three. In both planning and evaluation, more specific participation-promoting techniques may be applied as well, examples of which are life-cycle analysis, portfolio analysis, PEST (political, economic, social and technology) analysis, and SWOT (strength, weaknesses, opportunities and threats) analysis.

While strategic planning may commonly invite or even require broad participation, operational planning may be more difficult to make participatory, due to a common need for specific expertise, which only few people in the organisation may possess. Participation at this stage may also commonly be less significant, as questions addressed are often less fundamental for the organisation.

Participatory planning and evaluation in *local communities* may draw on a range of tools that have come to be grouped under the common heading of 'participatory rural appraisal (PRA)', which I prefer to refer to by the more broadly covering term 'participatory analysis'[13] or by the more recently used term 'participatory learning and action (PLA)'.

---

[13] The approach is applicable beyond what is commonly understood by 'appraisal' and may also be used in urban environments.

Depending on the type of development work and a range of contextual opportunities and constraints, examples of tasks that may be
accomplished as participatory processes may be:

- *village censuses*, which may cover a broad range of variables,
  examples of which may be house location, age and gender
  structure, employment structure, and health status;
- *ranking* numerous phenomena, such as the level of wealth of
  households, alternative facilities under a planned project, and
  benefits received from a programme or project;
- drawing *flow charts* and *task-actor diagrams* for organisational
  processes and responsibilities, in the past, present and/or future;
- *livelihood analysis*, for instance, comparing factors such as
  means of livelihood, food security, indebtedness, and locations
  of work before and after a development scheme, possibly for
  various groups;
- *time use analysis,* for instance, comparing different people's use
  of time before and after a development scheme;
- *mobility analysis*, i.e., mapping and explaining physical movements and, possibly, changes of these;
- brief *group exploration* of *specific phenomena* (natural, cultural,
  economic, etc.), possibly with emphasis on change;
- conceptualising and judging *future scenarios* through intra-group
  communication.

Community stories and *individual stories,* as presented by intended
beneficiaries or other stakeholders to a researcher, planner or
evaluator, may also be considered as participation-promoting tools,
in that they provide people's perspectives to persons or organisations who draw conclusions about or take decisions on development
matters.[14]

---

[14]   The readers may consult Dale (1998) and Mikkelsen (1995) for overviews
of participatory tools in those books themselves as well as for further references. Mukherjee (1993) is a rich source of examples of applications of
such tools.

3. BUILDING CAPACITY, ORGANISATIONS AND INSTITUTIONS

CONCEPTUAL FRAMEWORK

Augmenting the capability for development work and building organisations and institutions to that end are essential aspects of any broad development policy and strategy. Governments, non-governmental organisations and donor agencies have all tended to emphasise these dimensions more in later years than they did earlier. In line with this, 'capacity-building' and 'institution-building' have, as already stated, become important terms of the current development vocabulary. Connected to these terms is the somewhat less used word 'organisation-building'.

The three terms are often used vaguely and interchangeably. I will, in this section, make an effort to clarify them so far that they can be applied as useful analytical concepts in development studies, planning and more general communication.

Capacity-building may relate to people directly (to individuals or to non-organised groups), to organisations, and to institutional qualities of non-organisational nature.

When relating directly to **people**, capacity-building basically means to increase some personal capabilities. In the context of development, we may distinguish between two main notions:

First, capacity-building may mean to augment people's resources and other abilities for *improving their own living situation*, through own efforts. The resources and abilities to be augmented may span over many fields, such as: money, land, other production assets, health for working, vocational skills, access to information, understanding (of any issue relating to the person's living environment), and negotiating power.

In this perspective, capacity-building will normally, in the development sphere, apply to disadvantaged people, i.e., people who do not have capacities that they need for ensuring reasonable welfare for themselves and their direct dependants. We are, therefore, talking of *empowerment* of disadvantaged people.

In order to achieve empowerment, participation may be required (linking directly on to our notion of 'participation for empowering' in the previous section), but certain resources or measures may have to be directly provided by others. Examples of the latter may be allocation of land and curing of a debilitating illness.

Second, development agents may endeavour to augment capacities of individuals not for their own benefit or not primarily so, but *for the benefit of others*. An example may be training of health personnel, for the purpose of improving the health of the people whom this personnel is intended to serve. Another example may be promotion of entrepreneurship, through training of potential or existing entrepreneurs, for the sake of increasing production and employment in an area, to the benefit of people living there.

When relating to **organisations**, capacity-building may focus on a wide range of features and processes, addressed in Chapters Three and Four. Main examples are: policy – and strategy analysis; project planning; technology; management information systems; individual skills of various kinds; and issues relating to the organisation's form, culture and incentives.

In development work, capacity-building *of* organisations may, to larger or lesser extent, be done *by* some other organisation or organisations. When building (creating and/or strengthening) other organisations, the promoting organisation may augment capacity through *direct measures*, such as formal staff training, supply of office equipment, and improvement of work systems and routines. It may also supplement such measures with financial and other support for development work that is undertaken by the new or strengthened organisations. Under certain conditions, the latter type of support may be capacity-promoting as well, more *indirectly*, in that it may help the planning or implementing organisations learn from experience with the work that they do.

Some examples of programmes for building organisational capacity may be:

- a foreign donor agency strengthening a national government department for improving its policy and mechanisms of support for vocational training in the country;

- an international or national NGO building community-based Water Users' Associations to plan and implement small water supply schemes, possibly together with the NGO, and then to operate and maintain the schemes themselves;

- a regional development programme promoting local Savings and Credit Associations to generate savings and manage deposits and credit supply, rather than disseminating credit directly through its own organisational apparatus or through established banks.

Based on the above, we may simply define organisation-building for development as building the capacity of organisations for whatever development work they undertake or are involved in.

An organisation can be said to be institutionalised, i.e., to be an **institution**, when it is widely recognised, by those for whom it is or may be of concern (whether individuals or other organisations), as a distinguishable unit with its own legitimate role and tasks.[15] By this perception, all organisations that are formed or strengthened to undertake development work should be institutions as well or should definitely be intended to become so.

By direct implication, we can, when applying *this perspective*, consider all organisation-building for development as institution-building as well.

We may also distinguish between 'organisation' and 'institution' by *a different criterion*, whereby the latter extends beyond the concept of 'organisation'. The same would then apply to 'institution-building' in relation to 'organisation-building'.

For instance, an idea of 'institution-building for a more democratic society' may go beyond the formation or strengthening of organisational units (if at all incorporating building of organisations)

---

[15] See, in particular, Uphoff (1986). This connection between 'organisation' and 'institution' now seems to be a commonly accepted one.

to encompass aspects such as: formulating new national laws and regulations (for instance, regarding the permitted role of voluntary organisations); conducting training in democratic principles of governance; influencing attitudes of politicians; encouraging participation by a wider public in decision-making forums; and promoting freedom of the press.

Or, 'institution-building for poor people' in local communities may involve 'measures complementary to the building of organisations of poor people or organisations in which such people may participate. Examples of such related actions may be: assisting local government authorities to formulate new regulations for securing access by poor people to forests or other common natural resources; an information campaign aimed at influential people in the communities about contributions they may make for alleviating poverty; and promotion of interaction between people of different ethnicity or religions.

In broad summary, then, I propose that one clarifies distinctions made above by referring to relatively narrow and concrete efforts to strengthen organisations as 'organisation-building' and by referring to wider pursuits as 'institution-building'. In addition to any formation or functional strengthening of organisational units, such wider pursuits may include broader policies, laws and regulations, and various measures for empowering groups of people to participate in societal affairs for the purpose of sharing economic and social benefits. Examples of measures of the latter kind may be augmentation of deprived people's ability to participate in various forums, to form and manage organisations, or to play more significant roles in organisations to which they may already belong.

Additional points of summary of this section are that 'organisation-building' and 'institution-building' may both be referred to as 'capacity-building', and that the latter may in addition encompasses augmentation of individual abilities. Moreover, from the previous section we carry with us that participation may be an important or even necessary aspect of or condition for capacity-, organisation- and institution-building.

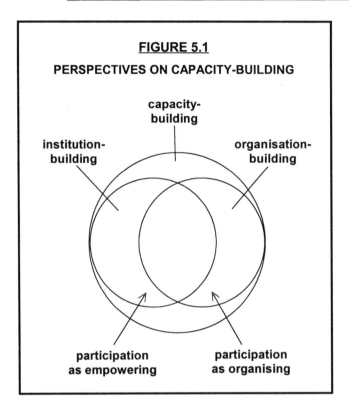

FIGURE 5.1

PERSPECTIVES ON CAPACITY-BUILDING

capacity-building

institution-building

organisation-building

participation as empowering

participation as organising

Main perspectives elaborated in the previous pages are also summed up graphically in Figure 5.1.

CONNECTING MEANS AND ENDS IN ORGANISATION-BUILDING PROGRAMMES

Virtually all work that we here refer to as 'development work' is organised; in other words, it is undertaken by one or more organisations in accordance with some organisation-based principles and regulations.

There has been a tendency over some years for more development work to aim at *organisation-building*. That is, a development organisation (or, in some instances, more than one organisation) helps create or strengthen other organisations. The purpose of such endeavours[16] is, then, to promote others to do development work rather than doing that work oneself. New organisations may be formed or the capability of existing organisations may be augmented.

Depending on how broad the perspective is, we may, alternatively, refer to such endeavours as *institution-building*. In the present context, we then assume that such institution-building efforts involve work with or within one or more organisations; that is, they take place within the overlapping space of 'organisation-building' and 'institution-building' visualised in Figure 5.1.

By conventional terminology, these new organisations or the augmented capability of existing organisations are most appropriately referred to as the *outputs* of the programme. Developmental achievements – *effects* and *impacts* – of such organisation-building programmes should then be viewed as the benefits created through the development work that the new or strengthened organisations undertake.[17]

For achieving such effects and impacts, the organisations that have been built will, of course, conduct *their* planning, implement *their* tasks, and produce *their* outputs. For analysing that work and those achievements we must, consequently, shift our focus from the support programme to the new or strengthened organisations.

This idea is visualised in Figure 5.2 overleaf. Being a further elaboration of Figure 4.1 (p. 124), this figure also summarises main components and arguments from other chapters pertaining to development work, of relevance for our argument here.

A programme-responsible organisation (or, in some instances, more than one organisation) decides on and operationalises a set of activities, through strategic and operational planning. In implementation, the organisation in charge converts the specified inputs into

---

[16] With reference to our discussion in Chapter Three, development endeavours of this nature should be referred to as 'programmes', not 'projects'.

[17] For further clarification of different terms relating to achievements of development work, see the last two sections of Chapter Three.

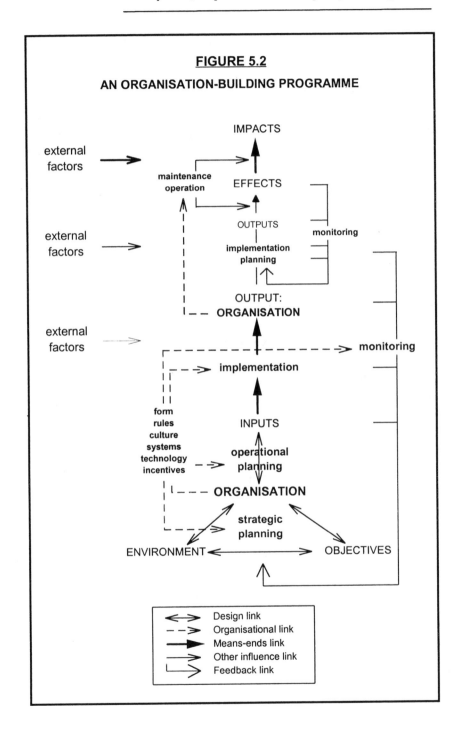

FIGURE 5.2

AN ORGANISATION-BUILDING PROGRAMME

outputs through the specified activities. In this case, the activities are organisation-building measures, with the wider purpose of creating some developmental achievements through the built organisations, as clarified above.

As elaborated in Chapter Four, the strategy, the operational plans, and subsequent activities of implementation and monitoring will be influenced or even largely determined by characteristics and abilities of the respective organisations (in this case the supporting organisation or the supported organisations, as the case may be). The features and performance of the respective organisations may be studied using the set of analytical categories of organisation that were presented in Chapter Four and shown in Figure 5.2 as well (although in the figure not repeated for the built organisations).

4. INSTITUTION-BUILDING AS PROCESS

All development work involves processes, in the sense that the outputs are created through chains of actions by sets of actors, both of which may be more or less complex. Additionally, the outputs generate effects and impacts through processes of change, in interplay with a range of external factors.

Institution-building may involve processes in particularly profound and diverse senses.

First, most institution-building measures produce outputs that are in themselves highly change-prone or dynamic (for instance, organisational units or individual knowledge). Second, this characteristic of fluidity tends to be caused by fairly immediate and strong exposure to varied and, often, changing environmental influence. Third, abilities on the part of organisations and other groupings (being normally the intended output of institution-building programmes) may be substantially influenced by feedback from work that these organisations and groups do, i.e., through learning from their own experience. And fourth, all these features of change and dynamism call for new-assessment and re-assessment by development agencies and workers, in the course of planning and implementation.

These dimensions of process are well illustrated through organisation-building programmes, addressed in the previous section: the built organisations are constellations of individuals with a range of interests, abilities and attitudes, some of which may also change frequently and substantially; the organisations become exposed to a variety of forces in their immediate and wider environment which may substantially influence their structure, other features of organisation, and mode of work; and they are expected to undertake development work, from which they will be gaining experiences from the very beginning.

Institutional outputs of non-organisational nature (such as laws, rules of procedure, and empowerment of individuals or groups) will normally be exposed to similar forces and be subject to similar feedback from practice.

In development planning and management, a recognition of the change-prone and generative nature of institution-building programmes is manifested in the planning mode of 'process', addressed in Chapter Three.

While *process planning* directly emphasises learning from planning and implementing development work (operationalised through interaction between planning, implementation and monitoring), such learning should also extend to the levels of effects and impacts, through generation of information about achievements and analysis of the multitude of factors that influence the outcome of the work done, including factors in the environment of the development scheme.

The basic rationale for process thinking, largely implied in what is said above, and further discussed in Chapter Three, is a recognition of greater *complexity* and a higher level of *uncertainty* than can be properly managed through blueprint planning. As stated by Mosse (1998), this involves an understanding and acceptance of unpredictable and idiosyncratic elements that are central to success or failure of programmes of this nature, making them not amenable to conventional prescriptive planning or management control based on pre-specified indicators of achievement.

The *external forces* which may influence the outcome of the respective programme, in the short and in the longer term, need to be identified and reflected on, with the aim of enabling the development organisation to relate to them as constructively as possible during its work.

This usually requires relatively current assessment of the types of forces at work, their strength, the kind of influence they exert or may come to exert, and how one may exploit opportunities they may represent or threats they may pose. We have earlier used terms such as 'strategic monitoring' and 'environmental scanning' to denote such frequent and flexible assessment.[18]

Moreover, in institution-building programmes, the interests, perspectives and influence of different *stakeholders* (some of whom may be considered as internal and others as external) are usually main uncertainty-promoting factors, the more so as such attributes or features may also change over time.

This perspective of process has, of course, implications for information collection for planning and management. Mosse (1998) mentions the following main characteristics, among some others, of *information management systems* for process planning and related modes of management (together referred to by Mosse as process monitoring):

- continuous (providing current information for deciding on any expansion, contraction or adjustments);
- orientation to the present;
- directly linked to action (being therewith also directed to participants who have the authority to react, as warranted);
- inductive and open-ended (enabling exploration of any events, relationships or outcomes – in contrast to conventional systems, which tend to be confined to examination of specified intended outputs or effects).

---

[18] For further discussion, see Chapter Three, Section 4 and Chapter Six, Section 2.

For many kinds of institution-building programmes, we may add to this list the feature of 'self-empowering'. With this is meant that the process of information collection and analysis promotes understanding and skills on the part of the participants which enable them to influence aspects of their life situation more than they could before, directly or more indirectly.[19]

The perspectives outlined above are basic for processes of development with broad participation of people, commonly referred to as *participatory development*. Programmes for promoting participatory development may involve devolution of responsibilities and relocation of work within government (local governance), intended to enable people to exert influence indirectly (through their representatives), or it may be in more community-based development endeavours, by which people participate directly, through their own voluntary organisations.

Programmes of this nature will virtually always emphasise organisation-building (whether of local government bodies or people's organisations). Moreover, institutional qualities and abilities in broader senses are frequently sought to be promoted through some form of facilitation, commonly involving what we will shortly (in Section 6) refer to as 'social mobilisation'.

We have already emphasised a general relationship between institution-building and process planning. Participatory development in a deep sense, involving empowerment through augmented organisational capacity and connected institutional qualities and abilities, may only materialise through iterative and generative processes of analysis, plan formulation, implementation and information feedback. That is, information generation, decision-making and action in the field are seen as closely inter-related activities, rather than clearly separated 'stages' of development work. This also means that development work occurs in small steps – through small projects or through projects that are broken down into phases.

---

[19] For a further elaboration, see Chapter Six, Section 7, on 'empowerment evaluation'.

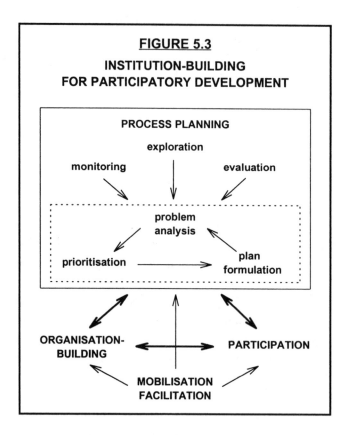

FIGURE 5.3

INSTITUTION-BUILDING FOR PARTICIPATORY DEVELOPMENT

A major contradiction in much recent development work has been between, on the one hand, ambitions of institution-building for participatory development and, on the other hand, continued emphasis on 'rational comprehensive' planning, constituting much of the scientific heritage of the planning profession. As clarified earlier, this planning mode (which, of course, may be appropriate in other contexts) requires specialised analytical skills (making the exercises basically top-down) and tends to lead to the formulation of comprehensive plans of basically blueprint character.

Figure 5.3 summarises main features of what we may refer to as the *organisation-building – participation – process planning nexus* in development. Iterative processes of problem analysis, prioritisation and plan formulation feed on information that is generated by the participants as integral parts of those processes – partly through exploration of any issue that may emerge as relevant and important, and partly through monitoring and evaluation of work that has been or is being undertaken. In the figure, all the components of the basic nexus are also shown to be supported by a built-in component of *mobilisation* cum *facilitation*.

For practical management reasons, planning will normally have to be structured in cycles (for instance, annual). This may still allow fairly continuous generation of information and learning.

5. ALTERNATIVE DEVELOPMENT, EMPOWERMENT AND GENDER

In Chapter Two, a distinction was made between the broad societal spheres of the state, the market and the civil society. Mainstream (neo-classical) economics analyses economic growth and develop-ment from the point of view of the market, most directly the firm. In reaction to this focus and the linked modes of analysis, John Fried-mann (1992) develops a concept of *alternative development*, being centred on 'the life spaces of civil society' (1992: 31), which he then connects to ideas of empowerment.

Within the civil society, the household is the core unit, composed of individuals who interact with others, inside and outside the household. The interaction is spurred by and itself promotes numer-ous needs, wants and obligations. Many of these can not be satisfied by or expressed through goods available in the market or through provisions by the state, although features of the market and the state may influence them. Instead, they must be understood primarily in the context of the civil society itself: obligations are influenced by moral codes, being culturally based, while basic psychological and social needs (such as affection, self-expression and self-esteem) arise from and get meaning through complex human interaction.

Alternative development is then seen as 'a process that seeks the *empowerment* [my emphasis] of households and their individual members through their involvement in socially and politically rele-vant actions' (Friedmann, 1992: 33).

The powers which may be thus augmented are of three kinds: social, political and psychological. Social power means access by household members to basic requisites for managing daily affairs, such as information, knowledge and skills, participation in organisations, and financial resources (some of which may be most appropriately considered to belong to the sphere of the market rather than the civil society). Political power refers to participation by household members in processes through which decisions about societal affairs are made, particularly decisions that affect their own future. Psychological power denotes potency in an individual sense, expressed as self-confident behaviour.[20]

This alternative perspective on development is, according to Friedmann, necessitated by what he refers to as the disempowering effects of the production-centred development paradigm. The new paradigm provides the basis for a strategy to counteract deprivation of large numbers of people and to promote development in a broad sense, emphasising the civil society context.

In particular, says Friedmann, the alternative development paradigm contributes 'a political dimension (inclusive democracy) as one of its principal ends of action' (1992: 34), 'acknowledging the *needs* and *established rights* [Friedmann's emphasis] of citizen households' (1992: 35).

Simultaneously, Friedmann recognises a need for continued economic growth and promotes his people-centred empowerment perspective as a supplement to, not as a substitute for, a production-centred one.

---

[20] Our earlier elaborated concept of 'participation as empowering' corresponds most directly to the political dimension, as presented by Friedmann. However, the three dimensions being usually closely inter-related, political participation will also be expected to have effects within the social and psychological spheres (as defined by Friedmann). Conversely, social and psychological power may be essential for increased political influence.

Our concept of 'capacity-building', as pertaining to individuals, encompasses empowerment in all the three senses stated by Friedmann.

These inter-relations will be better substantiated in the next two sections.

This perspective links well onto and amplifies our analysis of deprivation and development in Chapter One. The overall concern of that analysis, as well, was to promote a broad people-centred perspective on development, incorporating features and forces within the household and the civil society. To that end, a more specific and elaborate framework of deprivation and development was formulated than done by Friedmann, while the analysis of individual dimensions was less deep-ploughing.

Empowerment is a core theme in *gender analysis* (the analysis of relations between women and men).

At the levels of the household and the family, for instance, issues of empowerment have been explored comprehensively in studies with a gender focus. This is, of course, linked to the fact that the most basic intra-household or intra-family relation is normally that between women and men.

The more specific rationale for the empowerment emphasis in gender studies is the recognition that, virtually throughout the world, women tend to be discriminated against within the household and family. Commonly, even women who are household heads (normally in the absence of a husband) may have to relate to male kin on important matters, whether the men belong to the woman's household or are members of an extended family.

These asymmetric relations in the household and family have implications for the position of women in the wider public domain as well (Moser [1993]; Friedmann [1992]). Structures of subordination vary widely, but one can expect to find them in areas such as ownership and access to land and other means of production, division of labour, policies and legislation, in addition to more specific household and family affairs (Pearson [1992]).

Moser (1993), drawing on a framework by Molyneux,[21] makes a basic distinction between two kinds of women's needs (referred to by Moser as gender needs): 'practical' and 'strategic'. These two

---

[21] Molyneux, Maxine (1985): 'Mobilization without emancipation? Women's interests, state and revolution in Nicaragua'; *Feminist Studies*, 11 (2).

concepts are related to corresponding concepts of women's 'condition' and 'position', commonly seen in gender studies. Strategic needs directly reflect women's subordinate position to men. They 'relate to gender divisions of labour, power and control and may include such issues as legal rights, domestic violence, equal wages and women's control over their bodies' (Moser [1993]: 39). Practical needs are more immediately felt. They are identified by women 'in their socially accepted roles in the society' and 'do not challenge the women's ... subordinate position in the society ...' (1993: 40).

Empowerment relates most obviously and directly to strategic needs, because it is by combating subordination that women acquire greater influence over factors that shape their lives (being our broad definition of 'empowerment').

This does not mean that practical needs are necessarily low-priority ones. It may even be argued that it may be strategically wise to emphasise practical needs most. Friedmann (1992) speaks in favour of this. It is, he says, most feasible in the short term, in that it may enable involvement of relatively poor women from the outset in various development efforts. And, most fundamentally, it may initiate processes of change which may spread spatially and socially and induce gradual changes of more structural nature as well.

This view reflects an evolutionary and incremental perspective on development, in contrast to a revolutionary perspective, emphasising structural changes as the prime condition for economic and social improvements.

Without further discussing priorities in development work, it seems logical that both strategic and practical needs of women must be addressed, with due consideration given to the nature of women's problems as well as opportunities and constraints in specific situations.

The point may be substantiated with reference to the argument by Moser (1993) of a triple role of most women: reproductive work, productive work, and community managing. The reproductive part comprises 'the childbearing/rearing responsibilities and domestic tasks undertaken by women, required to guarantee the maintenance and reproduction of the labour force'; the productive part encompasses 'work done by both women and men for payment in cash or in kind'; and the community managing part involves 'activities undertaken primarily by women at the community level, as extension of their reproductive role ... to ensure the provision and maintenance of scarce resources of collective consumption such as water, health care and education' (Moser, 1993).[22]

The most constructive approach would seem to be parallel efforts in all the mentioned fields – albeit hardly by the same programme or project, at least in a planned integrated manner.

Such broad and diverse perspectives on changes may be important because aspects of the three spheres (reproductive, productive and community managing) are commonly inter-related, to larger or lesser extents. Consequently, changes in any one of the spheres, even of clearly practical nature, may influence the possibility to exploit opportunities in other spheres (or other opportunities in the same sphere).

For instance, easing the burden of reproductive work (through measures such as easier access to means of production, water for household use, health services or contraceptives) may facilitate involvement in household-external arenas. Simultaneously, basic structural conditions for such involvement (for instance, religious acceptance of public roles of women) will have to be fulfilled for this to occur. While some structures may be hard to change (among which fundamentalist religious tenets may be the most resistant ones), other structures (of belief, norms, laws, etc.) may be influenced and even substantially changed through changes in practical needs.

Deborah Eade (1997) presents an example of such a broad perspective on women's progress, by a set of 'status criteria' drawn up

---

[22] For further elaboration, see Moser (1993): 27–36.

The distinction between productive and reproductive work has been subjected to criticism, a discussion of which would lead beyond the scope of the presentation here.

by the Zambian Association for Research and Development. These include satisfaction of a set of basic material needs, leadership roles, increased consciousness about discrimination and women's issues, involvement in needs assessment and planning, restructuring the sexual division of labour, and acquiring control over factors of production (1997: 55).

6. SOCIAL MOBILISATION

'Social mobilisation' is commonly considered to be an important dimension of capacity-, organisation- and institution-building, particularly when relating to disadvantaged people.

I will, with Sylvie Cohen (1996), define social mobilisation as *a process of engaging a number of people in joint action for achieving societal goals through self-reliant effort.*

Social mobilisation may occur at all levels. Most often, however, the term is used for activities in local communities, although not necessarily confined to such communities. When thus confined, the process is commonly referred to as *community mobilisation.* This may involve whole communities or be limited to sections of communities (for instance, land-less people or groups of particularly poor women).

The process may be initiated, facilitated and co-ordinated by one or more persons, often belonging to some organisation, which is usually non-governmental. Common designations of these persons are *social mobilisers, community mobilisers, community workers, catalysts, change agents,* and *animators.*

When having a local community focus, main common <u>aims</u> of social mobilisation are, with varying emphasis:

- create *awareness* among community inhabitants, about structures and processes which influence their living situation negatively; about opportunities which may be exploited for improvements; and, commonly, about a development programme that the social mobilisation effort may be part of;

- build local *organisations* for developmental action, encompassing whole communities or specific intended beneficiaries only, or promote participation of disadvantaged or inactive people in existing organisations;
- strengthen people's *ability* to analyse their problems and possible solutions, and augment their individual and collective *skills* to undertake work for improving their living situation;
- help people who have little control over factors that influence their life to gain some decision-making *power* relating to such factors (for which organisation-building may be essential);
- through the above, promote people's *self-confidence*;
- mobilise people's own and other under-utilised or not utilised *resources*;
- establish *links* between community organisations and outside institutions, for various kinds of support from outside;
- establish *links* between similar organisations in different communities or, sometimes, promote higher-level *umbrella organisations* of community-based organisations.

Clearly, then, social mobilisation is primarily a mechanism of *empowerment*, although certain activities may not be directly empowering. It involves a broad range of measures for sensitising disadvantaged people about problems which they are faced with and the societal context of these problems; it commonly promotes organisation of the disadvantaged for increased strength and influence; and it usually involves practical advice and training for combating problems and improving the quality of life.

For effective empowerment, the social mobiliser should conscientiously try to abide by the following principles of work:

- *facilitate* processes of learning through soft while persistent mediation, avoiding directives from above;
- actively promote, even insist on, genuine *discussion* and *consultation* before decisions with implications for more than an individual are arrived at;

- promote engagement in *concrete development activities* which people can readily see the purpose of;
- act as a *liaison* person between weak local groups and outside institutions, while promoting the ability of the former to manage such relations on their own over the longer term;
- commonly, seek to promote suitable local persons for the role of *future change agents* in the communities.

In pursuance of these principles, the mobiliser should work in conformity with additional underlying principles of participatory development, mentioned in Section 2 of this chapter. Most essentially, the facilitator should approach each situation with humility, have a deep sense of respect for every participant, genuinely recognise local knowledge, and develop a capability to relate to complexity and uncertainty in a relaxed while purpose-conscious manner.

Although the emphasis should normally be on promoting people's own analysis and action, much social mobilisation incorporates elements of *advocacy*. That is, the mobiliser and the organisation which he or she represents want to promote some social values or development ideal.

Work among disadvantaged people to help them improve their lot – being very common in social mobilisation – is usually grounded on an ideal of greater social equality, and the advocacy element may become particularly strong when this involves organisation and other measures against oppression by other people.

Other examples of advocacy may be to promote adherence to some religious tenets, create greater sensitivity to and respect for ecological principles, and promote people's understanding of democratic principles of governance.

Development organisations and social mobilisers need to be highly conscious about the mix of advocacy and self-analysis in their mobilisation efforts, and they should clarify their attitude and approach in open discourse, both within their organisation and in their interaction with people who are or are intended to be beneficiaries of the organisation's work.

7. TWO EXAMPLES

I will illustrate the main concepts and issues that have been addressed in this chapter through two brief examples. The second example will also connect to earlier presented concepts of planning.

The first example is a kind of community focused development thrust that has come to be much emphasised lately. It aims at building people's organisations for broad-based development, frequently with savings and disbursement of credit as main components. The scope may be groups at the local level only or organisations in two or three tiers, in which local groups constitute the base.

These development programmes normally start with some awareness-enhancing and motivational work, the purpose of which is to make people more knowledgeable about and sensitive to social structures and forces of change in their society. Such *social mobilisation* is primarily intended to promote people's own reflection about problems afflicting them and their causes; however, as just stated, much such work contains an element of political activism or advocacy as well. The latter may also be needed in order to create sufficiently similar perceptions and ideas among the participants for common activities to be undertaken successfully.

This initial promotion of awareness and motivation for change, aimed at increasing the ability of individuals to conceptualise and subsequently act, is one form of *capacity-building*.

The initial capacity-building effort at the level of individuals soon gets intertwined with complementary efforts to build people's own organisations for challenging problems affecting the organisation's members; i.e., it will interact with *organisation-building*. This involves forming a set of organisations or organisational units in two or three tiers, and developing the necessary rules, codes of conduct and administrative systems for regulating the work of these organisations.

When pursuing their work, the organisations will mould the capacities of their individuals and various organisational features in producing their outputs, effects and impacts.

Moreover, as the organisations mature, the augmented abilities in interaction with the organisational structures and processes through which they get expression, will form a set of norms on which the organisations depend. The organisations will also project an image of themselves to their surroundings as bodies with their own legitimate roles and activities; that is, they become *institutionalised.*[23]

The promotion of this broad set of norms, organisational features and image (including 'institutionalisation' with the stated more specific meaning), along with related abilities to deal with other organisations and individuals and to address successfully a range of constraints and opportunities in their environments, is appropriately referred to as *institution-building.*

The latter means, then, that the initial awareness- and motivation-centred capacity-building will become part of a subsequent broader institution-building endeavour.

Incorporated into the concept of 'institution-building' (and, of course, the narrower one of 'organisation-building') will also be the promotion of other organisation-related capacities of the members than the ones mentioned above. Example may be guidance in strategy analysis and training in the management of the organisation's financial resources.

If savings and disbursement of credit are promoted, the members may usually take loans from their organisations for production enterprises that they, not their organisations, are in charge of. They may, additionally, get training relating to these enterprises.

Such additional capacity-building efforts, focusing on individual members for activities performed outside their organisations, fall outside the sphere of 'institution-building' (and therewith, of course, 'organisation-building'), as defined in this chapter. They would, in other words, be located outside the circles of 'organisation-building' and 'institution-building' in Figure 5.1. Still, such activities relating

---

[23] If institutionalisation does not occur, the organised units, although intended to undertake development work, may hardly ever be referred to as development organisations.

to individual members may be essential complementary measures, by more directly augmenting material benefits of the members.

The <u>second example</u> emphasises *aims* and *processes* of organisation-building. We here link to the concepts of strategic and operational planning that were presented in Chapter Three.

The scenario is a development organisation (for example, an NGO) designing a programme for creating new or strengthening existing development organisations in local communities.

The *outputs* of the programme will then be these local organisations, and the programme's *effects* and *impacts* may be seen as the benefits that are created by the local organisations for the intended beneficiaries in their communities, whether they are members of the organisations (which is most often the case) or outsiders.

Consequently, a clear distinction needs to be made between, on the one hand, the concerns of the development programme and the organisation or organisations responsible for that programme and, on the other hand, the concerns of the local organisations. We here focus on the former.

At the stage of *strategic planning*, the support organisation has to primarily address issues of *organisation*, within two different while interfaced spheres: the sphere of the local community and the sphere of the programme.

In the community sphere, it must decide on the type of organisations to be supported, features of these organisations, and the kind of people who may be involved in or with them (as members, beneficiaries and, possibly, resource persons). In the programme sphere, it must decide on the kinds, the magnitude, and the modalities of support to be rendered to the community organisations.

A key question is how uniform the programme wants the local organisations to be: shall they all be similar or can they vary to larger or lesser extents? The answer to this question will determine or influence important modalities of support, such as the degree of standardisation of the support, the degree of initiatives expected from the communities, and, consequently, the mode of communication between the support organisation and the communities.

Depending on the conditions which the programme establishes and the support it intends to provide, the support organisation may also have to deal with other strategy issues relating to the supported organisations, such as:

- *problems* of various kinds in different communities (for instance, to ensure that organisations are promoted in high-priority communities);

- *formulation of objectives* which are intended to steer the work of the local organisations;

- analysis of *external opportunities and threats* for the local organisations (for instance, to judge the likelihood of survival of the organisations or to assist the organisations in resisting or minimising threats).

Subsequently, the support organisation needs to conduct *operational planning* for its support, the scope, degree and modalities of which will depend on the strategy to be pursued.

Whether, in addition, the support organisation will plan anything operationally on behalf of the supported organisations depends on the extent to which it wants to steer or guide their work.

We have in this chapter focused on a range of issues relating to people's involvement in development work and on strengthening, through certain types of programmes, various kinds of abilities for promoting development. In doing so, we have distinguished between and separately analysed the concepts of participation, capacity-building, organisation-building, institution-building and empowerment. With this chapter, we have also concluded our exploration of planning and implementation of development work, having, in the process, addressed numerous issues of strategy and organisation relating to these pursuits. We now turn our attention to assessing the performance and achievements of development work that is being or has been undertaken, that is, evaluation.

Chapter Six

EVALUATING DEVELOPMENT ORGANISATIONS AND THEIR WORK

1. THE GENERAL SCOPE OF EVALUATION

Evaluation is undertaken in all spheres of life, informally or formally, whenever one wishes to know and understand the consequences of some action or event. What one learns from the evaluation is then commonly used to perform some similar activity in a better manner in the future.

Our concern is evaluation of planned and organised development work and of organisations involved in such work.[1]

Evaluation of development programmes and projects may be conducted during the implementation of the respective schemes or after they have been completed. Evaluation of development organisations may, in principle, be undertaken at any time during the organisations' active life.

---

[1] This chapter is partly based on a book I have recently written on evaluation of development programmes and projects (Dale, 1998).

The presentation here is angled to fit the general topic of the present book – development organisation and strategy. My evaluation book covers a wider range of evaluation topics, explores most issues more comprehensively and deeply, and illustrates topics and issues through numerous examples not incorporated here.

Development work centres on *people*, as substantiated earlier. Consequently, most evaluations of such work will also have people in focus. The most common rationale of development related evaluations is, thus, to document the utility for population groups of work that is being or has been done.

However, some evaluations of development work focus entirely or mainly on issues of strategy, organisation and/or operation. In such instances, the link to people may be indirect or even difficult to discern. Moreover, in order to explain effects and impacts for people, evaluators may have to devote substantial time to explore numerous organisational and operational issues, pertaining to planning, implementation and monitoring.

Other evaluations may address the general performance of one or more organisations or main parts of their work. With such a broad scope, the relation to people's well-being will usually be indicative only.

We need to view the programme, project or organisation under study in a *societal context*. That is, we can not limit the analysis to variables internal to the development scheme or organisation, but must in addition address relations between internal factors and numerous forces in the surroundings (environment) of the programme, project or organisation.

Formal evaluations of development organisations and their work should be conducted in a *systematic* manner; that is, they should be done conscientiously in accordance with a plan for the investigation, which should at least partly be specified before the evaluation starts.

2. EVALUATION IN INFORMATION – AND ACTIVITY CONTEXT

Commonly, evaluations contribute important and even essential parts of the total body of information that development organisations need for doing good work.

Generating and using such information is usually referred to as *information management*. It may involve: awareness about the types and amounts of information that are relevant and required; deciding on what information is needed by or should be accessible for units in the organisation and other stakeholders; deciding on who shall collect various types of information; means of collecting the information; means of processing the information; forms of documentation; and skills for collecting and processing information, along with training for acquiring those skills.

Information may be categorised by numerous criteria, such as: its *characteristics* (for instance, quantitative versus qualitative), its *purpose* (for instance, for planning or for organisation-internal administration), and *whom it shall serve* (for instance, the general manager, the technical supervisor, or external stakeholders).

Powell (1999) presents a useful classification, partly cutting across the just mentioned categories:

Activity-related information

This is a simple factual record of what is done, focusing mainly on implementation of planned activities. It tends to be of quantitative nature and may be intended for internal use or as basic information for outsiders.

Functional information

This information relates to day-to-day administration of the main-line activities of the organisation. It incorporates or draws on factual records (mentioned above) and may encompass financial analysis of various kinds, analysis of physical progress, etc., normally of quantitative nature. It primarily serves organisation-internal purposes, but may also be used by outsiders.

Management information

This is information that is used by the managers, for monitoring on-going activities (see shortly) and for planning new ones. It may be activity-related, functional or other (see immediately overleaf), but is often specifically tailored to serve management needs, through data combinations, summaries, etc. The information may be quantitative or qualitative.

Other information:

> This covers all information which does not fit into any of the above stated categories. It may be information, commonly of primarily qualitative nature, that is acquired occasionally or ad hoc in various ways, it may be contained in research documents, it may be feedback from a workshop, etc.

Activity-related, functional and management information is normally generated through formally planned systems. The systems are mostly designed and operated by the development organisation itself, but external bodies may also provide inputs to them and even assist in managing them.

In the development sphere, and also more widely, two main formal information generating systems are, as already stated, monitoring and evaluation. We have earlier also referred to them as two of the main 'functions' of development organisations. The two are additional or supplementary mechanisms to those for generating directly planning related information. They may be applied during the period of operation of an organisation, in the course of programme or project implementation, or, in the case of many evaluations, after the termination of the development scheme.

Yet another, much more specific and limited information generating mechanism may also be identified, namely 'appraisal'.

Before delving more into dimensions and issues of evaluation, we will use a couple of pages to clarify the main distinguishing features of the three just mentioned mechanisms.

In development terminology, <u>appraisal</u> is usually taken to mean *a critical examination of a proposal of a programme or project*, normally before this is approved for implementation and funding.

Monitoring and evaluation are both undertaken to find out how a development scheme or organisation performs or has performed. There are important differences between the two, although they are interfaced and commonly inter-phased.

Monitoring is, usually, the primary mechanism for generating activity-related, functional and management information, whereas evaluations may serve the purpose of generating supplementary management information and/or information of various kinds for external stakeholders and audiences.

Monitoring of *programmes and projects* was briefly mentioned in Chapter Four. Relatively current assessment of the execution of planned work (programmes and projects) is the most common notion of 'monitoring' in the development sphere. More concisely, I will define this as *frequent largely routine-wise collection and analysis of and reporting on information about the performance of the programme or project, comparison of this with the programme or project plans, and connected discussions about and proposals for any corrective action.*

Thus, monitoring of programmes and projects primarily aims at meeting the information need for current management of the respective development scheme.

Usually, monitoring of development work mainly covers matters of finance, the quantity and quality of inputs and outputs, and actors and time use in implementation. It may also (and commonly should) encompass some current assessment of direct results (effects), and may cursorily address additional issues of relevance and/or sustainability, which may possibly be analysed more thoroughly in some subsequent evaluation.

This form of monitoring is usually done, entirely or primarily, by the organisations responsible for the programme or project. There may be several persons involved in checking and reporting on various jobs, often at different levels of the organisations.

Most organisations, including those in the development sphere, will also have their internal systems for current assessment of *organisational performance* more generally, i.e., not directly or primarily relating to specific programmes and projects that the organisations undertake. Occasionally, such general monitoring of the performance of one or more organisations may be done by other organisations. Examples may be supervision of local government bodies by some central government department (being common in many parts of the world [see Chapter Two]), and continued gathering of information about the work of built organisations by the organisation-builder (see Chapter Five).

Organisation-internal monitoring may be done through the two co-ordination mechanisms of direct supervision and mutual adjustment,[2] usually in some combination. The mix of the two mechanisms tends to depend mainly on the form and the culture of the organisation (which, in turn, also tend to be inter-related).[3]

In addition, we may refer to a third, rather different, activity as 'monitoring'. This is relatively *current assessment of external (environmental) factors* relating to and influencing the performance of a programme or project or an organisation, coupled with analysis of and proposed responses to any important changes in relevant parts of the environment.

This is recognised as a crucial activity for success in the business world. It may be equally important in the development sphere, particularly in long-term programmes that are planned in the process mode, the more so the more open and the more complex these are. A suitable term for this activity is 'strategic monitoring'; another term, more commonly used, is 'environmental scanning'.[4]

---

[2] Mechanisms of co-ordination were addressed in Chapter Four, Section 8.

[3] There is an inclination to consider 'monitoring' as an activity that is performed through direct supervision only.

For most programmes and projects this is, clearly, the dominant mechanism, producing information about performance in some kind of recorded form. Even here, however, informal checks, usually of more mutual nature, and connected informal communication about what one does, how one does it, and whether things may be done differently are commonly more important than we tend to think.

Mutual adjustment, through informal inquiry, checks and suggestions, is commonly a very important mechanism for monitoring organisational performance more generally. In genuine collectives, it is the only mechanism for such monitoring, but even in quite rigid hierarchies it may be an important supplementary means to that of direct supervision.

[4] See Chapter Three, Section 4 for a further elaboration of 'environmental scanning'.

The concept of <u>evaluation</u> in development work will be further elaborated subsequently in this chapter.

For the moment, I will repeat the definition of the concept that was given in Chapter Four, by which it was broadly distinguished from 'monitoring', as *a more thorough examination, at specified points in time, of organisations, programmes or projects, usually with emphasis on impacts and additionally commonly on efficiency, effectiveness, relevance, sustainability and/or replicability.*

Evaluations may be done by members or staff of the organisation that is evaluated (often referred to as 'self-evaluation'), persons who are in direct charge of planning, implementation and/or evaluation of the programme or project that is evaluated, persons who are independent of the evaluated organisation or development scheme, funding agencies, groups of beneficiaries, or some combination of such people.

Evaluators usually draw on information provided through monitoring as well as additional information from a number of primary and secondary sources.[5]

Finally, in this section, I would like to clarify that the reason for emphasising evaluation in this chapter is that this function involves much more substantial and complex conceptual questions and issues than is normally the case for monitoring. When the information requirements to be met by monitoring have been identified and agreed upon, the remaining questions of designing and operating this function (pertaining to its organisation, recording systems, means of processing, etc.) are of mainly technical nature.[6]

---

[5] For definitions of 'monitoring' and 'evaluation', see also: Rossi and Freeman (1993), Rubin (1995), Germann et al. (1996), and Carlsson et al. (1994).

[6] This argument applies to monitoring in the sense of assessing the current performance of development organisations and schemes.

The third kind of monitoring mentioned above – strategic monitoring or environmental scanning – poses largely different challenges, of the nature addressed under strategic planning (in Chapter Three).

3. PURPOSES OF EVALUATIONS

In the perspective of the usage of the information that is generated, we may distinguish between two main types of evaluations: *formative* and *summative*.

Basic features and the general purposes of the two types are shown in Figure 6.1.

Formative evaluations aim at improving the performance and achievements of the organisation or scheme which is evaluated, through *learning* from experience. The possibility for feeding back new information form an evaluation to the same scheme may largely depend on whether we evaluate a programme or a project. For many development programmes, being of a framework nature, the scope for evaluations to induce changes of design and implementation may be substantial. For projects, the scope for changes may be limited to fairly modest adjustments, unless one concludes that the project must be re-planned – in full or in part.[7]

In addition to promoting the quality of work of the evaluated organisation or scheme through internal learning, formative evaluations may be a mechanism to ascertain the *accountability* of units and persons with various responsibilities in the respective organisation, programme or project. Involved people's perception of other involved people's adherence to rules and regulations, sense of responsibility and capability may strongly influence the general work morale and, consequently, work performance.

Formative evaluations are commonly done more than once. When that is the case, each exercise may not be very comprehensive. The evaluations may be done at set intervals or according to needs, as assessed by the responsible agencies. They may be managed and conducted by external persons, by persons working in the organisation or scheme, by beneficiaries, or by a combination of external and internal people.

---

[7]   See Chapter Three, Section 5 for a further elaboration of 'programme' and 'project'.

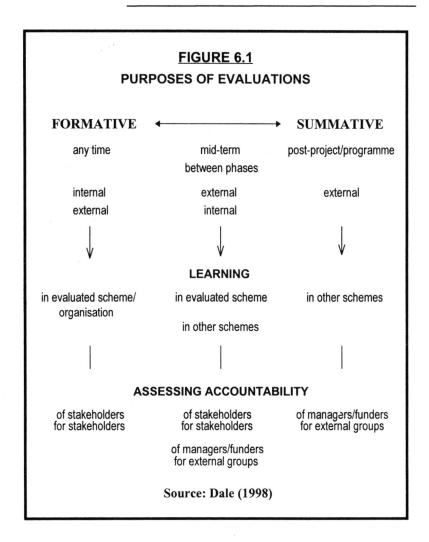

FIGURE 6.1

PURPOSES OF EVALUATIONS

FORMATIVE	◄—————————►	SUMMATIVE
any time	mid-term between phases	post-project/programme
internal external	external internal	external
↓	↓	↓

LEARNING

in evaluated scheme/ organisation	in evaluated scheme in other schemes	in other schemes

ASSESSING ACCOUNTABILITY

of stakeholders for stakeholders	of stakeholders for stakeholders	of managers/funders for external groups
	of managers/funders for external groups	

Source: Dale (1998)

Summative evaluations are primarily done of programmes and projects. They are undertaken after the respective scheme has been completed. Normally, their general purpose is to judge the worth of the evaluated programme or project and, along with that, the appropriateness of its design and management.

The experiences thus documented may constitute *learning* for planning and implementing similar development schemes. Usually, however, the more immediate concern is to assess the *accountability* of managers and possibly other stakeholders.

Summative evaluations of development work have been most common in developing countries, where they have largely been triggered by a need among foreign donor agencies to prove their accountability vis-à-vis their governments or other money providers as well as the general public in the donor country. For this reason, summative evaluations have also tended to be undertaken by persons who have been considered to be independent of the responsible programme or project organisations and the donor agencies.

Evaluations may also be conducted halfway through a programme or project (commonly called mid-term evaluations) or between phases of it. While the main purpose of evaluations thus timed usually is to provide information for any future adjustments of the same programme or project, accountability considerations too may be important.

Brief formative and mid-term evaluations are sometimes referred to as <u>reviews</u>.

4. A BASIC EVALUATION MODEL FOR PROGRAMMES AND PROJECTS

In Figure 6.2 are presented core features of Figure 4.1 (p. 124), which will be used as a *reference frame* for much of our discussion of evaluation of programmes and projects. To that frame I have connected the main concerns of evaluations. These concerns, which I will refer to as *evaluation categories,* appear in the figure in italicised capital letters.

The reference frame consists of a *strategy,* envisaged to have been worked out through an interdependent analysis of the variables spelt out in Chapter Three, and one or more *operational plans* based on that strategy. To this plan or these plans is then linked the basic *means-ends chain* of development programmes and projects, and influence from the *environment* is shown by arrows towards parts of the means-ends chain.

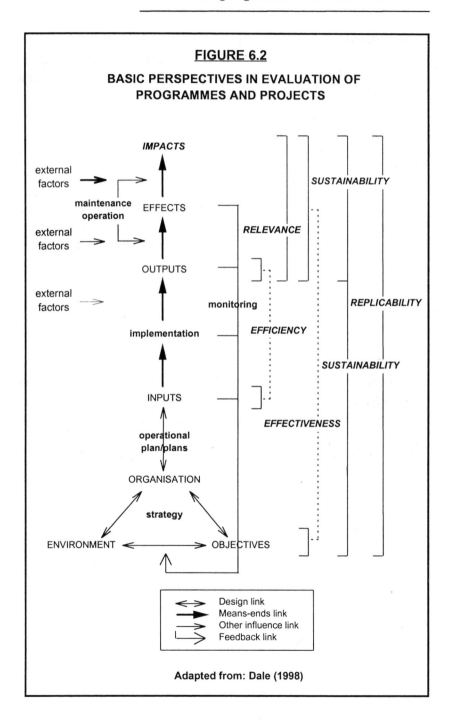

FIGURE 6.2

BASIC PERSPECTIVES IN EVALUATION OF PROGRAMMES AND PROJECTS

Adapted from: Dale (1998)

The stated evaluation categories constitute a set of main variables which evaluators are commonly expected to address. However, the terminology of different analysts and evaluators may not be entirely identical with that used in this chapter.

Below follows a brief elaboration of each of the evaluation categories appearing in Figure 6.2.

Efficiency

With this is meant *the amount of outputs created and their quality in relation to the resources (capital and personnel) invested.* It is, then, a measure of how productively the resources (as converted into inputs) have been used. This is shown in the figure by a link between 'inputs' and 'outputs'.

All inputs are usually quantified. The total cost of the outputs equals the sum of the costs of the various inputs that have gone into producing the outputs (which may include shares of general overhead costs).

For most engineering projects, one may estimate fairly objectively the amounts of various inputs which are reasonable for producing outputs of certain amounts and quality. For most other development schemes, this is usually not possible, and much subjective judgement by the evaluator may therefore be needed.

Such judgements have to be based primarily on circumstances and conditions under which the programme or project under evaluation has been planned and implemented. They may be further substantiated by experiences from the same or similar development work or by some theoretical reasoning.

Irrespective of the basis for such judgements, one will, for most societal development schemes, have to be satisfied with indicative conclusions only.

Effectiveness

Effectiveness expresses *to what extent the planned outputs, expected effects (immediate objectives) and intended impacts (development objective) are being or have been produced or achieved.*

This is shown in the figure by a link between 'objectives' on the one side and 'outputs', 'effects' and 'impacts' on the other side.[8]

In a well-planned project, the responsible organisation should be able to guarantee the outputs (although this may sometimes not be entirely realistic). The effects and the impacts will be influenced by external factors, to larger or lesser extent.

In practice, in effectiveness analysis, it may most often be appropriate to focus mainly on the *effects* on the outcome side, for the following reasons:

- the effect level is the first level at which benefits for the intended beneficiaries are expressed (directly or more indirectly), making effects a much more significant measure of achievements than outputs;

- being more directly derived from the activities of the respective programme or project than are impacts, the effects will normally be less influenced by intervening external factors and can therefore usually be assessed quicker and more reliably;

- thorough impact assessments, being commonly highly complex, may require a partly different methodology and may therefore most effectively be done additionally.[9]

Relevance

The issue here is *to what extent the programme or project is addressing or has addressed problems of high priority*, mainly as viewed by stakeholders, particularly the programme's or project's beneficiaries and other people who might have been beneficiaries.

The primary question may be whether the resources which are going into or have gone into the scheme might have been used with greater advantage for some *alternative development measures*.

---

[8]   Strictly speaking, by common development terminology, there are no objectives corresponding to the output level. Intended achievements at that level are more appropriately referred to as 'targets' than 'objectives'.

[9]   This argument is elaborated and substantiated in Dale (1998).

Closely related, one may ask whether it is the *people most in need* of the rendered assistance who receive or have received the benefits of the programme or project.

Moreover, for long-term development endeavours, a question that should commonly be asked is whether *original priorities* are still appropriate. If initial circumstances have changed, it may be warranted to change or in rare instances even terminate a development scheme before its completion.

Yet another question may be how well the programme or project *fits with other development work* which is or has been undertaken in the same area or the same field. Sub-questions may be whether it supplements such other work or instead overlaps with it, and whether it mobilises additional resources (local or external) or competes with others for the same resources.

Impacts

These are *the longer-term, largely indirect, consequences of the programme or project* for the intended beneficiaries and any other people.

The main impacts are, of course, expected to be positive. However, there may be negative impacts also, on beneficiary groups or others. These should be analysed as well.

Sometimes, negative impacts may have been suspected or even expected at the planning stage. These may then have been mentioned and even specified in the plan documents, with or without counteracting measures. In other cases, they may have been unforeseen. They may then also be more difficult to trace for evaluators.

Impacts are normally generated through complex relations and processes and they need, therefore, to be analysed through broad-focusing investigations.

Sustainability

This means *the maintenance or augmentation of positive changes induced by the programme or project after this has been terminated.*

Evaluators may assess the prospect for sustainability before or at the time of completion of the scheme, or they may, usually more reliably, assess or verify the sustainability at some later time.

Sustainability may relate to all the levels in our framework. It may, however, not always be relevant for the lower part of our model (the operational levels). That depends on whether the kind of development work which is being or has been done by the programme or project is intended to be continued after the termination of that intervention, through the same organisation or through one or more other organisations.

More specific examples of sustainability are:

- maintenance of physical facilities produced (such as a road);
- continued use of physical facilities (such as a road) or intangible qualities (such as knowledge);
- continued ability to plan and manage similar development work, by organisations which have been in charge of the programme or project or any other organisations that are intended to undertake the work;
- continued production of the same outputs (for instance, teachers from a teachers' training college);
- maintenance of impacts created (for instance, continued improved health due to new sanitation practices);
- multiplication of effects and impacts, of the same kinds or of other kinds, through inducements from facilities or qualities created by the programme or project.

Replicability

Replicability means *the feasibility of repeating the particular programme or project or parts of it in another context*, i.e., at a later time, in other areas, or for other groups of people.

This is an issue which may or may not be relevant or important. In some instances, replicability may be a major evaluation concern. That is most obviously the case with so-called pilot programmes and projects, that is, development schemes that aim at testing the feasibility or results of a particular intervention or approach. But replicability is important for all programmes and projects from which one wants to learn for wider application.

The replicability of a development scheme depends on both programme- or project-internal factors and environmental factors.

A replicability analysis may also include an assessment of any changes that may be made in the evaluated scheme in order to enhance its scope for replication.

5. INCORPORATING PLANNING AND ORGANISATION

In order to explain the performance relating to the categories elaborated above, the evaluator will normally have to address aspects of planning and how the scheme is being or has been organised.

As should have been well clarified, the lower part of Figure 6.2 (and of the earlier presented Figures 4.1 and 5.2) visualises an interrelated analysis of environmental factors, objectives, organisation and resources, through which a strategy is worked out and a subsequent operational plan is formulated and decided on. Together, these activities are referred to as planning.

Here, our additional concern is to examine aspects of planning in relation to the implementation and the achievements of the programme or project that is evaluated. The processes by which the plans have been generated (including actors in various roles, questions addressed, and how well the questions and emerging issues have been analysed) will have determined the appropriateness and quality of the strategic and operational plans, on which the further work depends, to larger or lesser extents.

In other words, the evaluator must judge how and to what extent the planning has influenced the quality of work and the results which are documented to have been obtained or are envisaged. All serious planning exercises will have their strengths as well as weaknesses, which may influence implementation and outcomes of the respective programme or project in many ways, positively or negatively.

The first step may be to find out who have actually participated in the planning effort and what the contribution of each of the actors has been. This may help trace whether all parties with legitimate interests have had a chance to influence the development work and also to judge whether people with appropriate expertise in relation to the tasks at hand have been involved or have been so to sufficient extents.

This should be interrelated with an assessment of various aspects of strategic planning, primarily: which problems have been in focus, how broad-based the strategy analysis has been, which problem-related issues have been covered, and how adequately the collected information has been analysed.

For further details about issues of strategic planning that may have to be addressed, the reader is referred to Chapter Three, Section 3.

Following this may be a similar investigation of the participation in and the coverage, procedures and thoroughness of the operational planning conducted, based on which the evaluator should ascertain the adequacy of the operational plan and how effective a guide for implementation it has been.

In Figure 4.1 (p. 124), the various dimensions of organisation – form, rules, administrative systems, culture, technology and incentives – were shown as influencing planning, implementation and monitoring and therewith in principle all the achievements of a programme or project. The mentioned organisational variables are in addition shown as influencing effects and impacts through organised operation and maintenance.

Obviously, evaluations will normally have to address such aspects of organisation as well. Commonly, they may have to be given major attention, as they may to various degrees explain achievements of the evaluated scheme.

For *visualisation*, these variables of organisation may be incorporated into our basic evaluation model (Figure 6.1) the way they appear in Figure 4.1, with no further changes to the model.

More specific organisational variables, additional to those shown in Figure 4.1, may also have to be examined. Main such variables, addressed in Chapters Four and Five, may be:

- leadership
- people's participation
- co-ordination
- personnel training.

Each of these, as well, may help explain outputs, effects and impacts. Consequently, they may also be important explanatory factors for findings relating to any of the other categories of evaluation that we have specified.

Additionally, one or more of the first three of the listed variables may be targets (intended *outputs*) of some programmes and projects, and may have to be evaluated accordingly.

This may most frequently be the case with people's participation, but even leadership and, probably less often, co-ordination may be incorporated into the set of intended outputs of development schemes, particularly programmes of building organisational capacity. In other words, member participation, leadership and co-ordination may be abilities that one aims at creating or augmenting in organisation- and institution-building programmes, discussed in Chapter Five.

People's participation may even be specified as an immediate objective (intended *effect*) of certain community-focused development programmes.

We now turn to the evaluation of programmes with such an organisation-building emphasis.

6. ORGANISATION-FOCUSED EVALUATIONS

EVALUATING ORGANISATION-BUILDING

In Figure 5.2 (p. 183) we modified and elaborated our basic planning and means-ends model, incorporating organisation-building as part of the means-ends chain. That figure visualises, in other words, a programme in which an organisation promotes other organisations to do development work rather than doing that work itself. New organisations may be established or existing organisations may be strengthened. Those organisational units and their new or added competence and capacity become, then, the *outputs* of the programme, as just reiterated.[10]

Commonly, as also stated in Chapter Five, the promoting organisation may combine direct organisation-building measures (such as formal staff training, provision of office equipment, and improvement of work systems and routines) with financial and other support for development activities undertaken by the new or strengthened organisations. The latter type of support may also have an organisation-building effect in that it may help the supported organisations learn from experience.

In Section 3 of Chapter Five, a few examples of organisation-building endeavours were presented. In Section 7 of the same chapter, two cases were further elaborated. For better understanding, the reader is referred to these.

For this kind of development scheme it is, as clarified in Chapter Five, reasonable to consider effects and impacts to be the achievements of the development work undertaken by the new or strengthened organisations.

---

[10] Development schemes of this nature are virtually always most appropriately referred to as 'programmes' (rather than 'projects'), following the terminology in this book.

Such endeavours are often referred to by development organisations as 'institution-building' rather than 'organisation-building'. This may usually be equally appropriate: as stressed earlier, organised units must become institutionalised for them to be referred to as development organisations. Whether we should use 'institution-building' rather than 'organisation-building' may also depend on the scope of the promotional effort, as discussed in Chapter Five. For the sake of keeping the presentation simple, I will not pursue this question more in the present context, but refer to the development endeavours addressed as 'organisation-building' programmes. The reader is referred to Chapter Five for a further discussion.

Evaluating such programmes becomes, then, largely a challenge of its own.

For studying the organisation-building endeavour itself, that is, for examining processes and outcomes up to and including the output level, the evaluator may proceed by exploring planning and implementation of the development work (in this case, organisation-building) in the manner clarified earlier. This may involve analysis of efficiency along with narrow conceptions of effectiveness (including only the output level on the achievement side).

However, for analysing effects and impacts and any of the other main evaluation categories that have been presented in the present chapter, the evaluator will have to turn his or her attention from the support programme to the work that the built organisations do, for which additional relations and means-ends chains will apply and need to be examined (see also the following sub-section).

For *visually* connecting our evaluation categories to the components of an organisation-building programme, we can just replace the simple means-ends chain in our basic evaluation model (Figure 6.2) with the more elaborate structure of Figure 5.2 (p. 183) – making sure that no changes are made in the relation between, on the one hand, the main means-ends components (from 'objectives' at the bottom to 'impacts' at the top) and, on the other hand, the evaluation categories.

EVALUATING ORGANISATIONAL PERFORMANCE

Figure 6.3 illustrates basic perspectives in evaluations that have the main focus on one or more development organisations, rather than programmes or projects.

The organisation is shown to link up with resources and connect to its environment for undertaking development work. Environmental factors will, in turn, influence the achievements of that work. The lines labelled 'development work' should be perceived as synonymous with the more elaborated means-ends chains in earlier figures; they have here been simplified to make the model easier to comprehend.

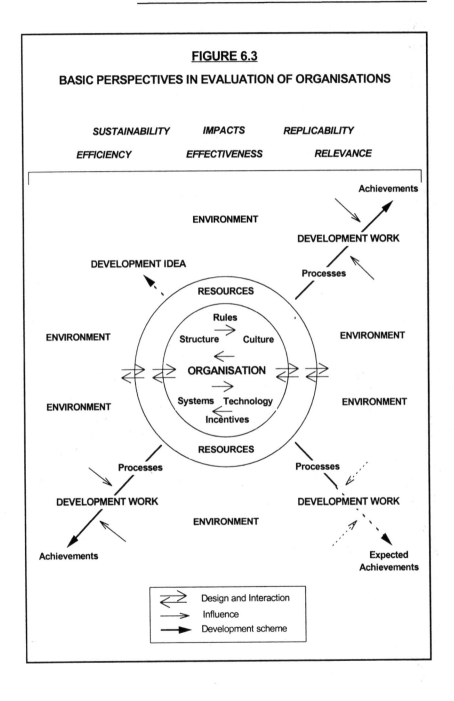

FIGURE 6.3

BASIC PERSPECTIVES IN EVALUATION OF ORGANISATIONS

Evaluations that focus on development organisations may be designed to *encompass*:

- the organisation's general vision and mission and the objectives of the work that it does, normally also including the kinds of beneficiaries whom it is working with or intends to work with;
- how the organisation analyses and deals with aspects in its environment, i.e., problems to be addressed and opportunities, constraints and threats;
- internal organisational features and processes;
- acquisition and use of resources;
- processes and achievements of the organisation's development work, with emphasis on underlying organisational requirements, mode of work and abilities.

The evaluation may be limited to one organisation or cover two or more organisations. In the latter case, comparison of features of the organisations and of the performance and achievements of their work may be a main purpose. This perspective is further elaborated in the last section of the present chapter.

Evaluations that focus on organisational performance can also be done as self-evaluations, sometimes also referred to as *internal evaluations*. This means that members of the organisation scrutinise their organisation's priorities, activities and achievements in a systematic manner, solely or basically for internal learning. Some kind of evaluation of one's organisation is usually done frequently or virtually continuously by people in the organisation, but the extent to which such exercises are conducted as formalised interactive processes varies greatly.[11]

---

[11]   For an account of internal evaluations, see Love (1991).

Other authors also address issues of internal evaluation, albeit under other headings. Informative while simple examinations in specific fields are undertaken by Drucker (1993) [on non-profit organisations] and Germann et al. (1996) [under the heading of 'participatory impact monitoring', partly relating to locally managed organisations].

Evaluations of organisations need to be very sensitive to and thoroughly analyse *changes* over time. This involves specifying the changes, explaining them (for which it is essential to sort between organisation-internal and -external factors), and analysing how the changes have affected the workings of the organisation.

Essential, more specific questions are to what extent the organisation has learnt from changes in its environment, and whether it has adjusted its vision and mission as well as its objectives, plans and modes of operation in response to such changes.

Another set of questions is how constructively the organisation has addressed internal conflicts that may have arisen and other internal crises that may have occurred, and what it has learnt from such conflicts and crises for its future pursuits.

7. EMPOWERMENT EVALUATION

Like planning and management, evaluations can, in themselves, be *empowering* processes. This idea is now getting expression through the term 'empowerment evaluation'.

Fetterman et al. (1996) specify core characteristics of empowerment evaluations as follows:

> The assessment of a program's value and worth is not the end point of the evaluation – as it often is in traditional evaluation – but part of an ongoing process of program improvement. ... Both value assessments and corresponding plans for program improvement ... are subject to a cyclical process of reflection and self-evaluation. Program participants learn to continually assess their progress toward self-determined goals and to reshape their plans ... according to this assessment. In the process, self-determination is fostered, illumination generated, and liberation actualized.

Thus, empowerment evaluations are of *formative* nature. As defined by Fetterman, they are also *internal* evaluations, i.e., conducted by people in the organisation themselves (see the previous section). The basic tenet is that empowerment can hardly be much induced by any external evaluator but must mainly occur through people's own systematic reflection, about work which is basically conceptualised, induced and controlled by themselves.

Still, evaluations with an empowerment rationale may often be fruitfully facilitated by outsiders. Such *external facilitation* may have a dual purpose: it may assist the participants in conceptualising and reflecting more deeply on a wider range of perspectives and ideas than they might from their own experience only, and it may help structure the process of evaluation itself.

In a development perspective, empowerment evaluation may be particularly significant for member organisations of poor or otherwise disadvantaged people. If such organisations encompass entire local communities or large sections of them, even whole communities may be empowered through the evaluation process.

Some empowerment of local community inhabitants may also be achieved through purposeful and active involvement by such inhabitants in evaluating development schemes in their communities that are managed, entirely or mainly, by external organisations. The empowerment may be manifested in increased knowledge and understanding which the participants may obtain in the very process of evaluation or, more directly, through increased subsequent benefits of the evaluated scheme for themselves. Conditions of the latter are that the evaluation is of formative nature and that the local people are able to influence the future priorities and arrangements of the programme or project.

Steven E. Mayer (1996) emphasises three *mechanisms* for allying evaluation of community development work with empowerment of the local communities:

- help create a spirit of participation in the evaluation, by
    - viewing outsiders and local people as 'co-discoverers';
    - viewing negative findings of evaluations more as inducements for improvements than as causes for punishment;
    - promoting a partnership of various stakeholders;
- directly include the voices of the intended beneficiaries, by

- incorporating their views about the purpose of the evaluation;
- incorporating their experience, wisdom and standards of good performance;
- including the most marginalised among them in the evaluation;

- help communities use evaluation findings to strengthen their responses, by
  - using various media to spread information and the lessons learnt;
  - helping to create links among people who may use the information;
  - helping community organisations to build on the experiences in their own further development endeavours.

8. DESIGNING EVALUATIONS

Over the next few pages, main aspects of the design of evaluations are briefly addressed. This section is to be seen as a supplement to the more substantive and, in the context of the present book, more fundamental dimensions and issues addressed so far. The emphasis is on suggesting a consistent and easily understood framework of the main analytical dimensions that evaluators have to consider and the range of methods which they may chose from for generating the information they need. For more in-depth exploration of design, including methods and techniques of data collection and analysis, the reader is referred to more specialised literature.[12]

---

[12] Among numerous publications, the following ones should be particularly useful, as well as easily accessible, in relation to evaluations: Dale (1998), Dixon (1995), Germann et al. (1996), Mukherjee (1993), Salant and Dillman (1994), and Casley and Kumar (1988). Among them, they cover the dimensions, issues and methods addressed here. For statistical analysis of data, reference is made to standard textbooks.

MAIN DIMENSIONS OF DESIGN

The Set of Study Entities

We may broadly distinguish between three main designs by the set of study entities incorporated:

- comparing the target population of the programme or project that is to be evaluated (or samples of that population) with a control group;
- comparing development organisations, programmes or projects;
- studying an organisation, a programme or a project without direct comparison with any other entity.

A *control group approach* is very common in the natural sciences, for experimental research. True experimental studies are done through collection of quantitative data and analysis of these, using statistical methods. If applied for development schemes, such experimental designs would be used for quantitative analysis of effects and impacts. Less stringent designs may also allow some amount of qualitative analysis of achievements.[13]

However, a genuine control group approach is rarely appropriate in evaluations of development work. That is, reliable conclusions about programme or project performance can hardly ever be drawn primarily from comparing changes in the programme or project population with changes in a control group.

This difficulty in comparing reliably between population groups is grounded on the fact that societal entities are complex constructs, in which numerous other forces than activities under the evaluated development scheme are at work, to larger or lesser extents. Such other forces will always create changes of various kinds, which will never be identical among two or more population groups and which will, therefore, disturb comparisons. In other words, development

---

[13]   A brief presentation of quantitative and qualitative designs follows a few pages ahead, along with an overview of the main methods under each of them.

organisations, and evaluators, are unable to control environmental factors of development schemes like a researcher can who works in a laboratory setting.[14]

In some instances, though, data about external groups may provide useful supplementary information, if carefully used in a non-experimental manner. This may sometimes justify incorporation of such groups in the evaluation design.

Comparison between development organisations and between programmes and projects are fairly common in evaluations. The purpose of this may be: to describe and explain differences in development priorities, types of development work and performance between similar organisations in similar environments; to analyse different approaches and achievements of different types of organisations in similar development work; or, probably most frequently, to trace and explain differences in implementation and achievements of similar programmes or projects in different environments.

Comparison makes sense only when it is based on a clear perception of similarities and differences (pertaining to the organisations or the development schemes, as the case may be). Whenever basic similarities can be identified, delimited and verified (i.e., whenever we know and can clearly show the basis for comparing), comparison may greatly help evaluators trace explanatory factors for performance.

We may, in principle, compare any variable under any of the evaluation categories that we have specified. Both qualitative and quantitative data may be collected, depending on the focus and breadth of the examination. Usually, however, it may be difficult to

---

[14]   A case presented by Fink and Kosekoff (1985) illustrates conditions that must be fulfilled for such an approach to be applicable in the social field. In their case, residents of a centre for elderly people were randomly assigned to one of three care programmes over a certain period of time, after which the quality of the three programmes, as assessed by the residents themselves, was compared. The core point is that the programme managers were able to establish strict control over the experiment through measures that prevented substantial influence by external factors.

undertake much statistical analysis of similarities and differences, as these may only rarely be sufficiently specified.

The most common approach in evaluations is to study the performance and achievements of individual organisations, programmes and projects *without systematic comparison* with other organisations or schemes. A main reason is that there may not exist entities (organisations or development schemes) that are sufficiently similar for systematic comparison to be made. Another common reason is that, although one might find reasonably comparable entities, the additional resources and time that would be needed for comparative analysis may be prohibitive.

Commonly, though, evaluators may be able to acquire some information of more indicative nature about other programmes, projects or organisations (whether identified prior to or during the evaluation) which may be of some help in the analysis.

Steps and Processes of Analysis

Another main dimension of design are the steps that one passes through and the processes that one indulges in in the course of the evaluation.

We may distinguish between four major approaches: before – after evaluation, retrospective evaluation, recurrent reviews and process evaluation.

<u>Before – after evaluation</u> primarily aims at studying benefits – expressed as impacts, effectiveness, relevance and/or sustainability of achievements. It involves examination relating to the intended target population (and, possibly, any control group) at two points in time: before the development scheme was started and after it has been completed. This is done in order to directly compare the 'before situation' with the 'after situation'. The examination should, of course, focus on features which are relevant to the particular intervention.

Such before – after studies are commonly referred to as 'baseline' and 'follow-up' studies or as 'pre-project' and 'post-project' studies respectively. Usually, household surveys, interviews with key persons, and/or some physical measurement are the main methods applied (see also later).

Most of the data that are collected in this way will normally be quantitative (expressed by numbers). Usually, the comparison is primarily made by entering the data pertaining to the pre- and post-situation in tables and calculating the differences between the values. Examples may be comparison of school enrolment rates, incidences of diseases, and income from some line of production.

More qualitative information may also be generated. A common example is people's perception or opinion about something, for instance, the adequacy of fuel-wood supply or the informants' utilisation of their time. To enable direct comparison between 'before' and 'after', such information must be recorded in some standard form (for instance, ranked). Certain qualities may even be judged by the evaluator based on direct observation, examples of which may be any differences in the standard of a road or the re-growth of vegetation on a protected piece of land. For such judgements to be reliable, both the before situation and the after situation should normally be assessed by the same person.

Conclusions about causes of observed changes between 'before' and 'after' are often based more on assumptions than on verification in the field. That is, one tends to conclude more from what one thinks is logical or reasonable than from an analysis of actual processes of change during the programme or project period and the factors that influence these processes.

One may, then, easily tend to conclude that all or most of any documented changes have been caused by the programme or project that is evaluated. In some cases, this may be highly likely or even obvious; in other cases, such judgements may be little reliable.

Consequently, one should, as far as possible, supplement before data and after data with exploration of processes and relations in the course of the programme or project period.

Retrospective evaluation may be done of programmes, projects or organisational performance. Most frequently, it is undertaken of programmes and projects after their completion. For long-lasting development schemes, it may occasionally be done at some stage during implementation. For organisations, retrospective evaluation may be done whenever there may be enough experiences accumulated by the organisation to look back on.

One may distinguish between two main variants of this approach. With the *first variant*, data about the before situation and the after situation are collected simultaneously, after the scheme has been completed. In its simplest form, the evaluator then compares the before data and the after data without much analysis of processes during the programme or project period and intervening factors. The focus is then primarily on impacts for intended beneficiaries (although most findings may rather be at the level of effects).

This may be seen as an impoverished equivalent of the 'before – after' approach, addressed above (impoverished because no baseline data were collected prior to programme or project implementation). Although much used in evaluations, this kind of retrospective analysis tends to produce little reliable information and may not provide much understanding of what has happened.

Increased reliability and greater understanding will, invariably, require an amount of analysis of processes and their causes. To the extent these are analysed, other main evaluation variables than impacts may be addressed.

Processes of change and influencing factors are emphasised in the *second variant* of retrospective evaluation. In this, there is no intention of acquiring a comprehensive data-set about the before-situation.

Instead, when emphasising programme or project benefits, the evaluator may start with documenting the after-situation and then work him- or herself backwards in time, for instance year by year, until sufficient information about changes and their causes are judged to have been obtained.

Alternatively, to the extent aspects of efficiency are in focus, the main or entire emphasis may be on operational aspects, during any part or parts of the planning and implementation period that the evaluator may be instructed or may decide to cover.

This approach may be chosen because before-data are not relevant. That is most obviously the case when the emphasis is on aspects of operation.

It may also be adopted because it may not be possible to obtain relevant data about the situation before the programme or project was started or because data that may be obtained are not considered to be reliable enough.

Moreover, even when studying achievements, the evaluator may not consider it necessary or worth the effort to collect baseline data, at least beyond some general pieces of information. A detailed record of processes and relations of change over some period may be viewed as more significant for documenting and understanding changes and for tracing and explaining the role of the evaluated programme or project in producing them.

For evaluations that go beyond an analysis of efficiency, this model may be particularly well suited for programmes, usually of relatively long duration, that set in motion diverse and complex processes of change.

Since one moves gradually from the present and well known to the more distant and less well remembered, the approach is also well suited in evaluations with people's participation, in which people together seek to bring to the surface information about the past, in the process discussing features and processes that have led to the situation they experience at the time of evaluation.

Examples of development schemes for which this model may be effective are many. Some of them are certainly: comprehensive community development programmes, group-based savings and credit schemes, production diversification programmes, and institution-building efforts of various kinds.

Analysis of operational performance and achievements of development organisations will normally have to be done retrospectively as well, emphasising processes of work, actors involved, and the interplay between numerous variables in the generation of outputs, effects and impacts.

Recurrent reviews are here defined as a system of flexible examinations of, in principle, any issue that may warrant attention in the course of implementation of development schemes, primarily programmes. Being a built-in component of programme design, reviews are intended to directly complement monitoring, i.e., to supplement the information that is generated routinely and relatively continuously by the latter. They are, then, a particularly flexible variant of formative evaluations, as earlier defined. They have also been referred to by names such as 'progress review' and 'diagnostic study' (the latter by Valadez and Bamberger [1994]).

Box 6.1 provides an example of how a system of recurrent reviews may be incorporated into and operated within a development programme. As illustrated by this case, this may be a particularly appropriate and effective component of long-term programmes that are, simultaneously, flexible enough for new initiatives and corrective measures to be taken, preferably within a framework of well structured process planning.

By their flexibility, individual reviews may address any aspect or issue under any of the categories of evaluation that we have specified. An exception may be rigorous impact analysis, which may require a methodology and an amount of time which may not be realistic for reviews. Still, even reviews may be designed in such a way that they may provide relatively reliable indications of benefits. One measure to that effect may be to conduct series of brief explorations with focus on the same population groups.

Process evaluation is here used to denote a vaguely delimited set of innovative perspectives and practices in the follow-up of development work. It may be more or less closely related to 'review', largely depending on how the system of reviews, if any, is designed and operated. Beyond frequent examinations, communication and related adjustments, 'process evaluation' embodies notions of openness, flexibility and broad participation. This is largely reflected in alternative concepts that are used, such as 'process monitoring' (Mosse, 1998), 'evolutionary monitoring' (Davies, 1998), and 'participatory impact monitoring' (Germann et al., 1996).

BOX 6.1

USING REVIEWS AS A MANAGEMENT TOOL
IN A PROGRAMME WITH PROCESS PLANNING

The Hambantota District Integrated Rural Development Programme (HIRDEP) in Sri Lanka, under implementation since before 1980, has been an unusually dynamic and flexible development endeavour. During the 1980s, in particular, it was operating according to a well elaborated model of process planning. A core aspect of this was annual programme documents with the following main features:

- review of the previous year's work and past experience;
- outline of a future strategy;
- proposals for new programme components (projects) to be started the following year;
- work programme for the following year, encompassing ongoing and new projects;
- indications of priorities (beyond already planned projects) over the next couple of years.

In the early 1980s, a flexible system of evaluations – termed reviews – was instituted, as a direct supplement to current monitoring, for feeding back information from ongoing and completed work into planning. Salient features of this system were:

- the focus and comprehensiveness of the reviews were situation determined and varied greatly;
- reviews could be proposed by any involved body (in practice mainly the overall planning and co-ordinating body, sector departments, and the donor agency) at any time;
- the planning of reviews was integrated into the above stated planning process, resulting in annual programmes of reviews;
- the review teams varied with the purpose, consisting of one or more insiders, outsiders or – commonly – a combination;

- a system of follow-up of the reviews was instituted, with written comments from involved agencies; a common meeting; decisions on follow-up action; and reporting on that action, mainly in the next annual programme document.

This system became increasingly effective over a period of a few years. It then disintegrated along with other management practices, due to changes of leadership and other personnel as well as strains imposed on the programme by the turmoil caused by an escalating ethnic conflict in Sri Lanka. When the programme was gradually revived, the programme concept came to be partly changed, primarily through a stated change of policy and new bureaucratic imperatives on the part of the donor.

Source: Dale (1998)

We are here in the borderland between monitoring and evaluation, and may, therefore, equally well refer to such activities by either of the two terms.

For further illustration, an outline is given below of Davies' specification of main features of an 'evolutionary' approach (1998: 77–81):

- seeking as much agreement as possible about the meaning of events towards the end of a process of information collection and analysis, the meanings being still subject to revision in the light of new experience (juxtaposed to more predetermined, firm and assumedly little controversial meanings with the 'orthodox' approach);

- trying to differentiate, by 'defining the meaningful edges of experience...' (rather than following the conventional norm of identifying a central tendency, mainly using techniques of quantification);

- applying inductive reasoning, by which indicative understanding is repeatedly abstracted out of recent experience (instead of deductive analysis based on an initial conception and initially established indicators);

- giving field staff and others closest to the experience that is monitored 'the right to pose to those above them a range of competing interpretations ...' (that is, allowing more processes 'from below', by the terminology used elsewhere in this book);
- 'parallel and distributed' processing of information (juxtaposed to analysis by a central body only);
- producing accounts of events that are richer in content than the statistical accounts which are produced centrally, placed in their local context, and in which the role of the observers and their subjectivity are visible;
- allowing monitoring to be dynamic and adaptive, reflecting 'both a changing world and a changing set of perceptions within the organisation ...' (juxtaposed to an unchanging focus and unchanging perceptions assumed in conventional monitoring).

Quantitative versus Qualitative Approach

A related dimension of design, already touched upon, is the basic nature of the data to be collected and the corresponding modes of analysis, commonly expressed as quantitative versus qualitative design. A quantitative design primarily produces information in numerical form while a qualitative design primarily generates information in non-numerical form and expresses findings mostly in words and sentences.

This has numerous connected implications. A typical quantitative approach is characterised by a pre-determined, unchangeable study design; it largely reduces the field of investigation to what is statistically controllable; and one tends to confine the study to the contemporary situation or to pre-determined points in time. A qualitative approach displays opposite features: it permits flexible and changeable study design; it may be broad-focusing and allows high complexity of research variables; and it enables direct analysis of processes. Qualitative methods may also enable greater participation by non-professionals – such as local community inhabitants – in the analysis. There are also other differences, of both conceptual and methodological nature, which will not be addressed here.

In evaluations, one should feel free to blend quantitative and qualitative methods, as they may often supplement each other in obtaining the best possible information most cost-effectively.

Generally, though, a primarily quantitative design (that is, application of a set of mainly quantitative methods) has strict limitations. If at all, it is mainly applicable for studying efficiency (through benefit-cost analysis), effectiveness (by comparing quantified targets with corresponding outputs and effects), and certain impacts. Usually, however, quantification is possible to only limited extents even for these categories: quantitative benefit-cost analysis has limited applicability in real-world development situations,[15] numerous intended and actual effects may not be expressed in numerical terms, and only fragments of the impacts that are generated by development programmes and projects may be quantified.

All other evaluation concerns, pertaining to our additional categories of relevance, sustainability and relevance, can only be meaningfully addressed in overwhelmingly qualitative terms. Any quantification would be limited to specific sub-matters only.

Thus, in broad conclusion, a primarily qualitative approach is required in most evaluations of development work. This may incorporate the collection of quantitative data and simple statistical treatment of these, for specific purposes.

Sources of Information

Another dimension of design is which sources of information the evaluator relies on. The most basic distinction is the one between primary and secondary sources. The information from these sources is, correspondingly, referred to as primary and secondary information (or data) respectively.

---

[15] For further elaboration and substantiation of this argument, see Dale (1998). For an easily accessible presentation of techniques involved, see, for instance, Nas (1996).

Primary information is most often provided directly by people. In evaluations, these are usually persons who have been or are involved in the organisation, programme or project that is evaluated or persons who are expected to have obtained some benefits. Primary information may also be acquired through direct observation or through measurement by the evaluator (in which case 'data' may be a more appropriate term than 'information').

Secondary information has already been produced by some other analyst, and may then be used by the evaluator for further analysis. The most common sources of secondary information for evaluators are monitoring forms and reports, other written documents, and occasionally maps.

MAIN METHODS FOR GENERATING INFORMATION

One may use a range of methods and techniques for collecting primary information or data.[16] These may be given different names and specified according to various criteria, and the resulting classification may be more or less complex.

For the present purpose, I will present a simple classification, distinguishing between four main categories of study methods, which I consider to be a useful framework for generating primary information for most purposes, including evaluation.[17]

Questionnaire survey

Several persons are here asked the same questions, the answers to which are then recorded in some pre-prepared format. This is a particularly useful method for studying effectiveness and impacts, and

---

[16] Selecting methods for collection of secondary information is much less problematic, and thus less of a scientific question.

[17] For further reading on methods of information generation, see literature referred to in footnote no. 12. For information analysis, the reader is referred to textbooks on statistics and qualitative design. In the present book, a brief overview of modes of analysing and presenting development related information is found in the last section of Chapter One.

often relevance and aspects of sustainability as well. This is because we commonly need information from a relatively large number of people to make reliable assessments of achievements in these respects. But the method may also generate information for analysing most other issues addressed in evaluations.

The questions, formulated in advance, may be closed or more or less open. That is, they may require precise brief answers or they may invite some elaboration, for instance, some judgement in the respondents' own words. Data or information in quantified or quantifiable form is then further processed statistically, whereas other information is analysed qualitatively (mainly in text form).

If applied to cover a large number of respondents in a short time (being commonly the case in evaluations), this method may not provide adequate understanding of important issues, because of limited opportunity to explore questions in depth, and often also because different persons may be employed to gather the information, restricting cumulative learning on the part of the analyst.

In-depth case study

This is a thorough and often long-lasting exploration, of local communities, population groups or organisations. Common sub-methods or techniques are: long formal (extended) interviews, in-depth semi-formal or informal communication with key informants, focused group discussions, and observation. Most of the information will be qualitative and requires further analysis of qualitative nature.

This is the best method for generating thorough understanding of complex relations and processes, pertaining to operation and even more to societal changes of various kinds.

The main drawback of the method is that it is usually more time-consuming than other methods.

Rapid assessment

This is the equivalent of what is more commonly called 'rapid rural appraisal (RRA)'. I use this alternative term because the method is equally applicable in evaluations as in appraisals and because it is suitable in many urban environments as well. This is a quick study. It is commonly undertaken by more than one person, each of whom may have different professional background and a prime responsibility for looking into specific matters. Broader judgements and conclusions are then normally arrived at through frequent communication between the team members.

More specific techniques include: quick observation, informal communication with key informants, brief group discussion, and checklist survey. The last is a brief questionnaire survey, where the questionnaire has the simple form of a list of questions or issues to be explored.

The mode of analysis is overwhelmingly qualitative.

Any evaluation issue may in principle be explored through rapid assessment. The main strengths of the method are that it may be done quickly, the unsophisticated nature of the techniques used, and its invitation to team-work. The main weaknesses are that information may not be widely representative and that it may not provide deep understanding.

Participatory analysis

This is also the equivalent of a more conventional term: 'participatory rural appraisal (PRA)'. A more recent term is 'participatory learning and action (PLA)'. It has lately come to be used as a common denominator of an array of techniques by which non-professionals may jointly explore problems, plan and evaluate.

In evaluations, participating people may be intended beneficiaries of programmes and projects which have been planned and implemented by others, or they may be people assessing the planning, implementation and outcome of development work over which they are or have been in full or partial command.

Main techniques are simple charting, ranking exercises, and oral accounts, including community stories and individual life stories.[18]

---

[18] For some further elaboration of tools of participatory analysis, extending beyond evaluation, see Chapter Five, Section 2.

Among the numerous questions that may be explored in evaluations through such techniques are: people's priorities (linking to relevance); the mission, portfolio and work processes of organisations; differences and changes in livelihoods; time use and any changes in this; changes in mobility; and past, present and future responsibility structure relating to development work (which may link to sustainability, for instance).

Commonly, it is preferable to use some combination of two or more of the above mentioned methods. For example, rapid assessment may be used to provide information that is needed for designing a questionnaire survey, or it may supplement the latter through a quick and more targeted exploration of some specific issue or a secondary population group. Examples of other useful combinations may be: a wide-covering questionnaire survey together with any of the other methods in selected communities or organisations; a broad rapid assessment together with participatory analysis in selected communities; and a rapid assessment together with an in-depth case study for exploring a specific issue.

REFERENCES

AIT NGDO Management Development Program (1998): *NGDO Management Development Training Manual;* Bangkok: Asian Institute of Technology (AIT).

Alexander, K. C. (1993): 'Dimensions and Indicators of Development'; *Journal of Rural Development;* Vol. 12, No. 3, pp. 257 67.

Analoui, Farhad (1993): *Skills of Management,* in: Cusworth, J.W. and T.R. Franks (1993: Chapter 5).

Aziz, Abdul and **David D. Arnold** (eds.) (1996): *Decentralised Governance in Asian Countries;* New Delhi: Sage Publications.

Biggs, Steven D. and **Arthur D. Neame** (1996): *Negotiating Room to Maneuver: Reflections Concerning NGO Autonomy and Accountability within the New Policy Agenda,* in: Edwards, Michael and David Hulme (1996).

Bryson, John M. and **Robert C. Einsweiler** (eds.) (1988): *Strategic Planning: Threats and Opportunities for Planners;* Chicago: Planners Press / American Planning Association.

Burke, W. Warner (1992): *Organization Development: A Process of Learning and Changing;* Reading, Massachusetts: Addison-Wesley Publishing Company (Second Edition).

Burkey, Stan (1993): *People First: A Guide to Self-Reliant, Participatory Development;* London and New Jersey: Zed Books.

Carroll, A. B. (1989): *Business and Society: Ethics and Stakeholder Management;* Cincinnati, OH: Southwestern Publishing.

Carlsson, Jerker; Gunnar Kohlin and **Anders Ekbom,** (1994): *The Political Economy of Evaluation: International Aid Agencies and the Effectiveness of Aid;* New York: St. Martin's Press.

Casley, Dennis J. and **Krishna Kumar** (1988*): The Collection, Analysis and Use of Monitoring and Evaluation Data;* Baltimore and London: The Johns Hopkins University Press (for The World Bank).

Chambers, Robert (1983): *Rural Development: Putting the Last First;* London: Longman.

———— (1993): *Challenging the Professions: Frontiers for Rural Development;* London: Intermediate Technology Publications.

———— (1995): 'Poverty and livelihoods: whose reality counts?'; *Environment and Urbanization,* Vol. 7, No. 1, pp. 173–204.

———— (1996): *The Primacy of the Personal,* in: Edwards, Michael and David Hulme (1996).

Cheema, G. Shabbir and **Dennis A. Rondinelli** (eds.) (1983): *Decentralization and Development: Policy Implementation in Developing Countries;* Beverly Hills: Sage Publications.

Cohen, Sylvie I. (1996): *Mobilizing Communities for Participation and Empowerment,* in: Servaes, Jan et al. (1996).

Crow, Michael and **Barry Bozeman** (1988): *Strategic Public Management,* in: Bryson, John M. and Robert C. Einsweiler (1988).

Cusworth, J.W. and **T.R. Franks** (eds.) (1993): *Managing Projects in Developing Countries;* Essex: Longman.

Dale, Reidar (1992): *Organization of Regional Development Work;* Ratmalana, Sri Lanka: Sarvodaya.

———— (1998): *Evaluation Frameworks for Development Programmes and Projects;* New Delhi: Sage Publications.

Dale, Reidar (1999): 'Regional Development Programmes: From Prescriptive Planning to Flexible Facilitation?'; Paper; Pathumthani, Thailand: Asian Institute of Technology.

―――― (2000): 'People's Development with People's Money: The Mobilisation–Organisation–Finance Nexus'; Paper; Pathumthani, Thailand: Asian Institute of Technology.

Damelio, Robert (1996): *The Basics of Process Mapping;* New York: Quality Resources.

Davies, Rick (1998): *An Evolutionary Approach to Organisational Learning: An Experiment by an NGO in Bangladesh*, in: Mosse, David, John Farrington and Alan Rew (eds.): *Development as Process: Concepts and Methods for Working with Complexity;* London: ODI and Routledge.

Dixon, Jane (1995): 'Community Stories and Indicators for Evaluating Community Development'; *Community Development Journal,* Vol. 30, No. 4, pp. 327–36.

Drucker, Peter F. (1993): *The Five Most Important Questions You Will Ever Ask About Your Non-profit Organization;* San Francisco: Jossey-Bass Inc.

Dusseldorp, D.B.W.M. van (1981): 'Participation in Planned Development Influenced by Governments of Developing Countries at Local Level in Rural Areas'; *Essays in Rural Sociology;* Wageningen Agricultural University.

Eade, Deborah (1997*)*: *Capacity-Building: An Approach to People-Centred Development;* Oxford: Oxfam.

Edwards, Michael and **David Hulme** (eds.) (1992): *Making a Difference: NGOs and Development in a Changing World;* London: Earthscan Publications.

―――― (1996): *Beyond the Magic Bullet: NGO Performance and Accountability in the Post-Cold War World;* West Hartford, Connecticut: Kumarian Press.

Faludi, Andreas (1973a): *A Reader in Planning Theory*; Oxford: Pergamon Press.

Faludi, Andreas (1973b): *Planning Theory*; Oxford: Pergamon Press (New edition 1984).

Farey, Peter (1993): 'Mapping the Leader/Manager'; *Management Education and Development,* Vol. 24, Part 2, pp.109–21.

Farrington, John and **David J. Lewis (eds.)** (1993): *Non-Governmental Organizations and the State in Asia: Rethinking Roles in Sustainable Agricultural Development;* London: Overseas Development Institute / Routledge.

Fetterman, David M., Shakeh J. Kaftarian and **Abraham Wandersman** (eds.) (1996): *Empowerment Evaluation: Knowledge and Tools for Self-Assessment & / Accountability;* Thousand Oaks, California: Sage Publications.

Fink, Arlene and **Jaqueline Kosekoff** (1985): *How to Conduct Surveys: A Step-by-Step Guide;* Newbury Park, California: Sage Publications.

Friedmann, John (1992): *Empowerment: The Politics of Alternative Development;* Cambridge, Massachusetts: Blackwell.

Friend, John and **Allen Hickling** (1997): *Planning Under Pressure: The Strategic Choice Approach*; Oxford: Butterworth-Heinemann.

Friend J.K. and **W.N. Jessop** (1969): *Local Government and Strategic Choice: an Operational Research Approach to the Processes of Public Planning*; Oxford: Pergamon Press.

Galbraith, Jay R. and **Robert. K. Kazanjian** (1986): *Strategy Implementation: Structure, Systems and Process*; St. Paul: West Publishing Company.

Galloway, Dianne (1994): *Mapping Work Processes;* Milwaukee: ASQC Quality Press.

Germann, Dorsi; Eberhard Gohl and **Burkhard Schwarz** (1996): *Participatory Impact Monitoring;* Eschborn: Deutsche Gesellschaft fur Technische Zusammenarbeit (GTZ) – GATE (Booklets 1–4).

Green, Andrew and **Ann Matthias** (1995): 'Where do NGOs Fit In? Developing a Policy Framework for the Health Sector'; *Development in Practice,* Vol. 5, No. 4, pp. 313–23.

Grimble, Robin and **Man-Kwun Chan** (1995): 'Stakeholder Analysis for Natural Resource Management in Developing Countries'; *Natural Resources Forum,* Vol. 19, No. 2, pp. 113–24.

Handy, C.B. (1983): *Understanding Organisations;* Harmondsworth: Penguin.

Hunt, Diana (1989): *Economic Theories of Development: An Analysis of Competing Paradigms;* Hertfordshire: Harvester Wheatsheaf.

Iddagoda, Kusum S. and **Reidar Dale** (1997): *Empowerment through Organization: The Social Mobilization Programme in Hambantota, Sri Lanka;* Pathumthani, Thailand: Asian Institute of Technology.

Keough, Noel (1998): 'Participatory Development Principles and Practice: Reflections of a Western Development Worker'; *Community Development Journal,* Vol. 33, No. 3, pp. 187–96.

Kliksberg, Bernardo (1997): 'Rethinking the State for Social Development'; *The International Journal of Technical Cooperation,* Vol. 3, No. 2, pp. 163–91.

Korten, David C . (1987): 'Third generation NGO strategies: A Key to People-Centred Development'; *World Development* Vol. 15, pp. 145–59.

Love, Arnold J. (1991): *Internal Evaluation: Building Organizations from Within;* Newbury Park, California: Sage Publications.

Mackintosh, Maureen (1992): *Questioning the State,* in: Wyuts, Marc et al. (1992).

Mayer, Steven E. (1996): *Building Community Capacity With Evaluation Activities that Empower,* in: Fetterman, David M. (1996).

Mikkelsen, Britha (1995): *Methods for Development Work and Research: A Guide for Practitioners;* New Delhi: Sage Publications.

Mintzberg, Henry (1983): *Structures in Fives: Designing Effective Organizations;* Englewood Cliffs: Prentice-Hall International (New edition 1993).

———— (1989): *Mintzberg on Management: Inside Our Strange World of Organizations;* The Free Press.

———— (1996): 'Managing Government: Governing Management'; *Harvard Business Review*, May–June, pp. 75–83.

Moris, Jon and **James Copestake** (1993): *Qualitative Enquiry for Rural Development: A Review;* London: ODI.

Moser, Caroline O. N. (1993): *Gender Planning and Development: Theory, Practice and Training;* London and New York: Routledge.

Mosse, David (1998): *Process-Oriented Approaches to Development Practice and Social Research*, in: Mosse, David; John Farrington and Alan Rew (eds.): *Development as Process: Concepts and Methods for Working with Complexity;* London: ODI and Routledge.

Mukherjee, Neela (1993): *Participatory Rural Appraisal: Methodology and Applications;* New Delhi: Concept Publishing Company.

Nas, Tevfik A. (1996): *Cost-Benefit Analysis: Theory and Application;* Thousand Oaks, California: Sage Publications.

Oakley Peter et. al. (1991): *Projects with People: The Practice of Participation in Rural Development;* Geneva: ILO.

Pearson, Ruth (1992): *Gender Matters in Development*, in: Allen, Tim and Alan Thomas (eds.) (1992): *Poverty and Development in the 1990s*; Oxford University Press.

Pongquan, Soparth (1992): *Participatory Development Activities at Local Level: Case Studies in Villages of Central Thailand;* Wageningen Agricultural University.

Porras, Jerry I. (1987): *Stream Analysis: A Powerful Way to Diagnose and Manage Organizational Change;* Reading, Massachusetts: Addison-Wesley Publishing Company.

Powell, Mike (1999): *Information Management for Development Organisations;* Oxford: Oxfam.

Pratt, Brian and **Peter Loizos** (1992): *Choosing Research Methods: Data Collection for Development Workers*; Oxford: Oxfam.

Pugh, Derek S. and **David J. Hickson** (1997): *Writers on Organizations;* Thousand Oaks, California: Sage Publications.

Rosenau, Milton D. Jr. (1992): *Successful Project Management: A Step-by Step Approach with Practical Examples;* New York: Van Nostrand Reinhold.

Rossi, Peter H. and **Howard E. Freeman** (1993): *Evaluation: A Systematic Approach* (5th ed.); Newbury Park, California: Sage Publications.

Rubin, Frances (1995): *A Basic Guide to Evaluation for Development Workers*; Oxford: Oxfam.

Salamon, Lester M. and **Helmut K. Anheier** (1997): *Defining the Nonprofit Sector: A Cross-National Analysis;* Manchester: Manchester University Press.

Salant, Priscilla and **Don A. Dillman** (1994): *How to Conduct Your Own Survey;* New York: John Wiley & Sons, Inc.

Scott, W. Richard (1987): *Organizations: Rational, Natural, and Open Systems;* Englewood Cliffs: Prentice-Hall International.

Servaes, Jan; Thomas L. Jacobson and **Shirley A. White** (eds.) (1996): *Participatory Communication for Social Change;* New Delhi: Sage Publications.

Shotton, Roger (1999): 'Policy and Institutional Analysis and Programming Strategies for Local Development Funds'; *Regional Development Dialogue,* Vol. 20, No. 2, Autumn 1999, pp. 160–72.

Thomas, Alan (1992): *Non-governmental Organisations and the Limits to Empowerment,* in: Wuyts et al. (1992).

Uphoff, Norman (1986): *Local Institutional Development: An Analytical Sourcebook With Cases*; West Hartford, Connecticut: Kumarian Press.

―――― (1996): *Why NGOs Are Not a Third Sector: A Sectoral Analysis with Some Thoughts on Accountability, Sustainability, and Evaluation*, in: Edwards, Michael and David Hulme (1996).

Uphoff, Norman et al. (1979): *Feasibility and Application of Rural Development Participation: A State of the Art Paper;* Cornell University Ithaca: Rural Development Committee.

Valadez, Joseph and **Michael Bamberger** (1994): *Monitoring and Evaluating Social Programs in Developing Countries: A Handbook for Policymakers, Managers, and Researchers;* Washington D.C.: The World Bank.

Waters, Donald (1996): *Operations Management: Producing Goods and Services;* Harlow: Addison-Wesley Publishing Company.

Wickramanayake, Ebel (1993): *How to Identify Projects;* Bangkok: Asian Institute of Technology.

Wuyts, Marc; Maureen Mackintosh and **Tom Hewitt** (eds.) (1992): *Development Policy and Public Action;* Oxford: Oxford University Press.

INDEX

ABOUT THE AUTHOR

Reidar Dale is Associate Professor of Rural and Regional Development Planning at the Asian Institute of Technology (AIT), Pathumthani, Thailand. He started his career as a research fellow and teacher at the University of Oslo. He was then, for two decades, engaged in development research and practical development work in various capacities, before joining AIT in 1995. Main fields of involvement have been policy analysis, integrated rural development, community development and micro-finance, with emphasis on strategies and aspects of organisation and management.

As adviser and evaluator, Reidar Dale has been working with organisations such as the Norwegian Agency for Development Cooperation (NORAD), Redd Barna (Norwegian Save the Children), Sarvodaya (Sri Lanka), the United Nations Capital Development Fund (UNCDF), and the Food and Agriculture Organisation of the United Nations (FAO).

Reidar Dale has previously published the following books: *Evaluation Frameworks for Development Programmes and Projects*; *Empowerment through Organization: The Social Mobilization Programme in Hambantota, Sri Lanka* (co-author); *Organization of Rural Development Work*; and *Sri Lanka: Country Study and Norwegian Aid Review* (co-author). He has in addition published articles and written research reports and papers on a variety of topics.